IN THE MIDST OF WINTER

by Louise Hageman, O.P.

STUDIES IN FORMATIVE SPIRITUALITY

Volume One

General Editors:

Adrian van Kaam, C.S.Sp., Ph.D.
Bert van Croonenburg, C.S.Sp., S.T.D.
Susan Annette Muto, Ph.D.

Preface by Adrian van Kaam

Louise Hageman, O.P.

President of the National Sisters Formation Conference

Dimension Books · Denville, New Jersey

Volume One: *Studies in formative Spirituality*

Dimension Books
Denville, New Jersey 07834

First Edition Published by
Dimension Books, Inc.
Denville, New Jersey

CONTENTS

Page

General Introduction 5

Foreword 11

Introduction 15

Part I—SUFFERING—A SOURCE OF INWARDNESS *"In the midst of winter . . ."*
Chapter I—Creative Suffering 21

Part II—SELF-ALIENATION-PSEUDO ESCAPE FROM SUFFERING ". . . *I* . . ."
Chapter II—Psychological Alienation 27
Chapter III—Cultural Alienation 39

Part III—BECOMING A PERSON THROUGH AUTHENTIC RESPONSE TO SUFFERING ". . . *finally learned* . . ."
Chapter IV—Suffering as Warning 47
Chapter V—Suffering as a Condition for Refinement and Depth 54
Chapter VI—Suffering as a Means of Communion with Others 62
Chapter VII—Suffering as a Means of Purification 67

Part IV—SUFFERING IN RELATION TO THE SACRED ". . . *that there was in me* . . ."
Chapter VIII—The Religious Nature of Person 73
Chapter IX—Distorted Religious Suffering 79

Chapter X—Positive Value of Suffering for the Religious Person 91

Part V—CHRISTIAN SUFFERING "... *an Invincible Summer.*"

Chapter XI—A Christian Incarnates God In This World 102

Chapter XII—Christian Suffering As Lived by Augustine 114

Epilogue 130

Footnotes 131

Selected Bibliography 143

GENERAL INTRODUCTION

The Christian today has entered a new era of history characterized by rapid change. The time of a monolithic Church civilization is over. The Christian enclaves of medieval Europe will never return. The ghettoes have broken open and we are exposed to other views and forms of life. Faced as we are by a bewildering number of options, it seems difficult to relate them to our inner life direction in Christ.

In a world of increasing choices, we find ourselves often confused about how to grow to our graced destiny in the Lord. The secular world is dynamic, fascinating, seductive. Beguiled as we sometimes are by its grandiose projects, we begin to grow according to its arbitrary enthusiasms rather than growing as self directed Christians in accordance with divine inspirations. We become so adept at reacting we forget how to respond out of an inner at-oneness with the Lord and his word. We try to adopt new life styles, to be in with what is current. We define ourselves mainly on the basis of our occupations and hobbies or on how our neighbors value us. We become our secular roles to gain the approval of the world and betray the Christian in us who has to penetrate and transfigure these roles. We take on new patterns of living, yet we do not try to harmonize them with our spiritual values. We slide along thoughtlessly, bewitched by the media, beguiled by the sophistication of our secular peers.

Propelled by our need for self emergence, in accordance with the times, we forge ahead often in directions that have no real meaning for us because they are at odds with our inner direction. We lose our concrete sense of self and, the more lost we become, the more desperately we search for substitutes. In our desire to emerge and become what we are called to be, we may rush after every fad that offers a quick solution to the spiritual quest.

While present day secular society is a confusion of paradigms and life styles, it offers at the same time an astonishing variety of incarnational possibilities; it enables Christian spirituality to reveal itself in a richness of forms undreamt of before. Because of this pluralism of life styles, more types of Christians can live out their unique destiny; they can find their peculiar niche in the Father's house where those many rooms promised by Jesus are now becoming manifest. We may have lost security and simplicity, but we have gained creativity and pluriformity. The uniform Christian culture may be dead, but Christianity itself seems more alive than ever.

Since it is no longer sustained by a universal Christian culture, Christianity is like a leaven spreading itself through the dough of a redeemed humanity, transfiguring countless cultural styles and forms with the words and wisdom of Christ, incarnating itself in myriad ways in this world. Creative self unfolding in Christ has become a much more personal endeavor. The secular society offers no guidelines for authentic inner growth; only Christ and the masters of the spiritual life, who lived in his light, tell us what is involved in spiritual emergence in dialogue with the ever changing word where he calls us to be his "little flock."

The purpose of these studies in formative spirituality is to contribute to this dialogue. The publications in this series will direct themselves to various dynamics of the Christian life, illuminated for us in scripture and tradition, that gain in depth of meaning when placed in dialogue with newly emerging insights in literature, human sciences, and the contemporary experience of man. Each study intends to help the Christian find his life form in this unsteady and bewildering age. Each intends to help us answer such basic questions as: How can I find my way as a creative Christian in the new, wide open situation of a diaspora Christianity? How can I live the essential message of the faith in my own style now that there is no longer a uniform cultural code to tell me in detail how to incarnate Christ in my life and my world?

Christian spirituality can be seen as a discipline that guides this search for spiritual identity. The words of scripture, the teaching of the Church and her spiritual masters, illumine this pursuit. They inspire attitudes enabling us to be more open to the call of our true self in Christ. Spirituality explores these attitudes; it examines how we prepare for them, how they transform our daily life. When spirituality is approached in this practical way, it is called formative spirituality.

The focus of the formative approach is on the conditions, structures, and dynamics of Christian unfolding in daily life. It wants to facilitate the graced discovery and unfolding of our destiny in Christ. This new field of study tries to establish the necessary and sufficient conditions for our personal-spiritual formation. It examines from this perspective special and personal spiritualities, experiences, devotions and exercises, abstracting in this way the essentials. It attempts to provide the Christian with a lasting foundation for graced living in Christ; it helps him to find his own practical and particular solutions to the life questions he will have to face without betraying the fundamental conditions of a Christian spiritual life.

This approach also takes into account the psychological, social and physiological obstacles that may interfere with the discovery of our true life form or life direction in Christ. Similar obstacles may hinder the full permeation of our whole life and personality by grace. The human sciences contain findings and insights regarding such obstacles and suggest effective ways of coping with them. Formative spirituality integrates—and if necessary transforms—such insights along with those found in Church doctrine, scripture, spiritual theology and philosophy into a self consistent approach to the personal-spiritual formation of the Christian.

Formative spirituality is in this way profoundly practical, for it refers to what effects a change in the inner life of the Christian. Change of a superficial nature effects mainly the emotional, psychological or external surface of personal life; profound change effects a lasting inner conversion. Formative spirituality tries, therefore, to discover, describe and apply the principles of the process of a profoundly practical change by grace. In this way it wants to be of help to Christians who go through conversion experiences at various successive stages of a deepening of their life by grace.

Formative spirituality builds on a theory of the development of the human person in relation to the invitation of grace. Contributions from such fields as the biblical and historical study of spirituality, the critical-textual approach to spiritual masters, and the systematic theology of spirituality are taken into account whenever advisable or necessary, but they are not the prime focus of this new field, which is to assist Christians in the discovery and unfolding of a unique life form rooted in their human make-up and in the specific direction grace gives to their lives.

During fifteen years or more of developing this specialty,

the results have been most gratifying. The vast majority of students, after three years of study and preparation in this field, have spontaneously reported on profound changes they experience in their personality and in the people entrusted to their care. The studies presented in this series have been written by men and women who for a prolonged period of time have participated in the unfolding of the new discipline of formative spirituality at the Center for the Study of Spirituality at the Institute of Man at Duquesne University. It is our hope that this series will enable the reader to participate in the fruits of this new field of study and to become a little more aware of the dialogue and deepening to which each Christian is called.

The Editors

FOREWORD

It is my pleasure to introduce the first book of this series of studies in formative spirituality. The author, Sr. Louise Hageman, has studied this new field with genuine interest and dedication. For three years, during her stay at the university center of which I am director, she elucidated one aspect of formative spirituality in the light of the methodology developed by this approach to human life. The topic she selected was suffering. She was guided by the faculty to reflect on the nature and meaning of human suffering and to ponder how it could be truly formative if lived creatively. Next her studies focused on the obstacles to creative suffering and the alienations that could emerge due to psychological and cultural factors that would turn us away from the fruitful acceptance of suffering in our lives.

In accordance with the integrative principles of formative spirituality, she was asked to explore what scripture and the spiritual masters have taught us about suffering and to bring their vision in dialogue with her own experience, with that of her contemporaries, and with philosophical and psychological writings by present day authors. All describe this basic human challenge and the many ways in which we can cope with it. After this research, the author was able to plumb the depths of the religious and Christian meaning of suffering.

It is most gratifying that Sr. Louise Hageman took the time and energy to select from her extensive study and its ample documentation those sections that are interesting to an audience not at home in this new discipline but eager to receive some of the experiential and practical insights engendered during her three years of research. The result of her work is this well written, attractive book that may foster reflection in the reader on the inescapable mystery of suffering. This book may also give readers an entrance to this new approach to spirituality. The side of life so well described by Sr. Louise is fundamental for all of us, especially today when we are so inclined to escape suffering or to cover it up with pious platitudes. She tells us instead about the concrete meaning of this experience for our personal and Christian growth and about how to meet this challenge concretely in everyday living.

Of course, suffering is not the only challenge that comes to meet us, no matter how basic this experience may be. Therefore, readers should look forward to forthcoming books in this series—books based on the same theoretical-experiential principles of formative spirituality. Sr. Louise's book, together with others in this series, will help to build a well rounded library that addresses the quest for personal and Christian living in today's world.

Adrian van Kaam

IN THE MIDST OF WINTER

Louise Hageman

"In the midst of winter I finally learned that there was in me an invincible summer."
Albert Camus

ACKNOWLEDGEMENT

I dedicate this book in gratitude and love to my religious community, the Sisters of St. Dominic, Great Bend, Kansas. I am particularly grateful to Sister Jeanette Sulzman, Sister Celine Benoit and Judy Menke who helped refine the manuscript and continually encouraged me and to my faithful typist, Sister Jane Marie McCoy.

I wish also to express my sincere appreciation to the faculty of the Institute of Man, particularly to Father Adrian van Kaam and Doctor Susan Muto, for their interest and assistance at the time of my study in Duquesne.

Finally, I am grateful to my family and friends without whose inspiration and love this work could not have been accomplished.

INTRODUCTION

Four years ago at the Center for the Study of Spirituality of the Institute of Man, Duquesne University, I completed a thesis on suffering. In the process of writing I discovered that, although I began this study thinking I had never really suffered, I had had suffering experience. Both of my loved parents had died; loneliness had been a rather constant companion and suicidal thoughts, which in their very clarity made me break into a cold sweat, stalked my life.

Mostly though, I denied all these and many other suffering realities. I lived my life in anxiety. This anxiety was both unrecognized and unnamed.

Writing, studying, and reflecting about suffering confronted me with the fact that I had never really lived my sufferings. In the three years that I spent researching the topic and trying to explore my own experience, I changed. I could not mouth words I did not live and at the same time experience any sort of wholeness.

I realized that I was alienated, out of touch with myself. I was caught in the consumeristic, competitive, materialistic milieu in which I lived. The divine spark within was dying. I had become so embedded in emptiness that I believed "that is all there is." In fact, I was too empty to really suffer.

To some degree, I still am. I keep waiting to write this book because I feel it is so incomplete; nonetheless, I have come to realize that all things human take time and that though my search will always be unfinished, I need to write.

What happened was, that though fearful of the unknown, I was forced to look for a harbor, a shelter from nothingness, and in the process I was partially released from my prison. The will to live was born by subjectively passing through death. As I entered my self alienation, my emptiness, my nothingness and named my questions, life grew free and in this freedom my creative, alive self was discovered.

Before me hangs a poster with a quote from Bach's *Jonathan Livingston Seagull* which reads, "We're free to go where we wish and to be what we are." Is freedom related to alienation? Are we free? Can we be free? Most of us want to be free. But perhaps when we first experience our freedom we are like the bison in the film, *Bless the Beasts and Children* and we don't go very far i.e. we do not actualize our potential, because like the bison, we do not yet know how to use our freedom. We may be our own greatest enemy.

We get caught in the need to be liked so we become people pleasers, or the need to get ahead and we penny pinch, or the need for attention and we sit on our pity pots. But we are made to be free to go where we wish and to be what we are or, as someone said so simply with tears in her eyes, to smell the grass. Why then, do we so often go where we would not and be what we are not? True, Christ told Peter, that he would be led where he would not wish to go but the paradox is that in going there, Peter, was given back to himself. Here, we speak of going not because He calls but because we are so absent from the truth of our life, that we are manipulated into what we would not.

Unfortunately most of us are unaware that we are living in an alienated fashion. Can we change this pattern? Do we want to change it? If we never realize our imprisonment, we are not free to change because we do not know that we are only half living. One trend, that predominates in our society and that futurologists predict will increase, is self-alienation.

Look with me, and see if there is truth in what I say. Are we not bored, living the sameness of life in a stale and lifeless way? By lifeless, I don't mean quiet. I mean lifeless. Quiet is often filled with life. In fact my proposition is that we have so little life because we have so little real quiet . . . real inner calm in which we dare to look at truth. As long as we keep running, we need not listen. I believe that if I am to be my creative real self, I must grow in authentic inwardness.

Creative living springs from an inner unique force, from something deep within that makes me most myself. To live creatively is to discover my inward person. It means entering deeply into my inner well and freeing what is there, what is me and, yet, more than me. Living creatively means finding my own deepest truth and since it is truth, it means touching the truth of all, the ground of all reality, the Ground of Being.

The biblical teaching rings true, "the Kingdom of God is within." Only by coming in touch with my deepest self can I go through and beyond myself to the Self that sustains us all.

How do I grow in inwardness? Mostly, I find it hard just to be with my self unless some experience moves me to inwardness. One such experience can be the experience of suffering. In this book I am going to share some of my research and reflections on suffering. Most of these reflections are presented in dialogue with philosophical, psychological, sociological, and literary works. Correlations, commonalities and implications are demonstrated.

It is true that I can discover only some of suffering's kernel, just as I can only playfully glimpse what creative living means. I may make dogmatic statements but they are far from dogma. It is only in a leisurely search into reality that truth emerges. By listening and dialoguing with what is written here, truths deep within yourself may be discovered that move beyond what is recorded.

Hence, rather than try to develop a line, I will spiral into my subject, touching again and again the same bases and hopefully, with each spiral facilitate a deeper penetration into truth. The three bases or aspects around which these reflections revolve are inwardness, limitation and attitude. The inwardness we experience in suffering discloses our limitations and in this inner reflective stance we determine our attitude.

In conclusion, the following journal reflection highlights how Scripture parallels the personal experience described in this introduction.

> "Have not joy and gladness vanished from the house of our God." Joel 1:16
> "But now, now—it is Yahweh who speaks—come back to me with all your heart." Joel 2:12

DARK ROOMS

My heart is lonely.
Many dark rooms are within,
Life holds little promise
It's all been done before.
Offices, places to go, things to do,
Even hours with friends, turn
empty-shallow-repetitive-lifeless.
Why? Why do I, who usually feel that
all of creation is full of promise,

find myself scared, scared of my own aloneness,
my deathlike inner world?
Is this a call, a call to go deeper
  into the rooms, the passageways
  dark—dark—?
But then the darkness becomes familiar,
  life even lingers here, I think.
Is that you, Yahweh?
Am I asked to suffer my existence
To discover richer, truer,—yes more
Honest Life?
Then fearfully, not too energetically,
but really, I hope, I live "Yes."

PART I

SUFFERING A SOURCE OF INWARDNESS

"In the midst of winter . . . "

CHAPTER I

CREATIVE SUFFERING

She is dead. Often I had feared this moment. I knew she saw the doctor weekly. Once in the middle of the night I heard the priest with her. The following morning I kept silent waiting to learn if any of the family whose mumbling voices I recognized the night before would tell me about the anointing. They did not. I decided that I would have to investigate for myself to find out what I really did not want to know. When she took her daily nap on a couch in the back room, I would creep to the door, open it a crack to check if she were still breathing. After I had seen her chest rising and falling rhythmically I could run and play, knowing I would have her a while longer.

But now she is dead. I am without a mother. In one way, it is a relief. The long waiting is over. My life becomes a rather serious one. I spend hours sitting in the corner of the garage or walking alone and lonely. Yet, I want to be by myself. I have to think, to find direction for my life. I don't want to be lonely, but there is no one to whom I care to tell everything. I shared so much of my life with my mother. Now I am learning what it is to be without her.

Her absence throws me back on myself and I turn within. I realize that no one can replace her. I will have to stand on my own. My life can never be the same. In a sobering fashion I know that I myself am responsible for me. I cannot depend on outside guidance because no one cares for me in the same way. Her death is something that has happened, and I cannot change it. I feel that I can never be totally happy because separation from those I love will always be a possibility. I am limited. Furthermore, I too, will die. I cannot avoid pain and death, but I can choose to live this one life, my life, in the best way.

When we are confronted with suffering, we don't like it. We want to get out of it in any way we can. We want to alienate the pain from ourselves. Maybe if we get busy enough, or find some jolly good fellows, or simply go to sleep, the remembrance of the suffering will go away. At some point, however, all is quiet, and the skeleton of denied reality peeps out. Perhaps we pretend that the anxiety is not there. But pretense leaves us with an unsettled, restless, rotten feeling. All is not right but we dare not look. We say and live that which is not ourselves. We will not admit that we are aliens to ourselves because as long as we ignore the truth, we need not assume the responsibility to change. However, if suffering gets painful enough we may be forced to remain with it. We may for the first time really be honest about life or we may be cynical, bitter and/or indifferent.

Suffering is an evil. In the sense, though, that suffering moves me toward inwardness, toward truth, toward reintegration of selfhood and thus refines and deepens me, suffering is gift.

Let's suppose that you—I—become gravely ill. I see the doctor and from his conclusion I realize that things are bad. I can't believe it. This kind of thing only happens to other people. Not to me. What am I to do? At first people write or call or take time to visit but with time it seems that my illness becomes a matter of indifference for most people, maybe because they, too, are scared of death. After awhile, even my friends seem bored when I tell them about my pain. I am left alone with it, with myself; but I am scared to be alone. I go to my room and lie down, I get up, there is nothing I can do to change this painful reality. The days pass and the pain increases and I alone know of it and all those about me don't understand or don't want to understand, and they go about as if everything in the world is as it was before. I reflect. "I shall be no more, so what will there be when I am no more? Is this death? No, I don't want to die."

So, we are terrified about being alone and yet we feel that anything is better than death. What makes this aloneness so hard to bear is our inability to face who we really are, what our lives are all about. We have lived so long away from our real selves that we are not aware that we live a lie. When we can quit defending ourselves and let go of self-righteousness, when we can be with ourselves and enter deeply, courageously into our inner world, then we move toward truth—the truth of who we are. And it is this very truth that sets us free. Through it we transcend a past that has not been all that it should be. Maybe for the first time, we may bring together all our real values and experience a sense of wholeness. We may find the courage to ask forgiveness and to sincerely care for others, all others. Death loses its terror and though physically we may be dying, in a deeper sense we are reborn and know a oneness with reality that brings real joy.

Must we wait until faced with our own or another's death before we know such oneness with reality, such freedom? Can we be free to actualize the full potential of ourselves long before we face the immediate reality of death? How? It is in the inwardness, the awful aloneness of suffering, that we face truth. Can we take this journey inward without suffering?

Dag Hammarskjöld has an entry in his diary *Markings* which reads:

> The longest journey
> Is the journey inward
> Of him who has chosen his destiny
> Who has started his quest
> For the source of his being.[1]

The journey inward is a long one. To enter deeply into the inner well, to have some kind of inner life, to be in solitude is initially foreign. We are restless. What, after all, can come of this? It seems that we are doing nothing. Certainly, we have produced nothing concrete in solitude. Doesn't the American way demand that we have something to show for ourselves, that we be practical, and forget interiority?

Such may be our critique of a solitary life style. If we continue to listen to our remarks, we discover that similarly we are saying, "Why don't you talk with him, I never seem to really come across like I want to. I get defensive, etc. . . . " Or, we may supposedly get along well with all kinds of people and yet experience ourselves as restless. Is this because we do not know ourselves?

Hammarskjöld says if we choose to know this "I", to know our destiny, our truth, if we are in quest of the Source of our being, we must go within. We must take this painful inner journey to truth.

Each of us must discover our own unique way of entering this inner world of ourselves. Today, some are finding that the intensive journal of Ira Progoff facilitates such presence to one's self. A journal certainly can be a means of seeing deeply into truth and such reflective insight is indeed a form of contemplation. There are multiple ways we may experience inwardness. Sometimes it may be in nature, in music, in relationships, and all of these can be some form of contemplation.

To contemplate is to be in communion with. It is to wonder in order to discover the ultimate root of reality. When we thus commune, we are no longer cut off or alienated from life. According to Douglas Steere, contemplation is described as the power to look steadily, calmly, and searchingly at something. Or, as Aquinas says, contemplation is a simple unimpeded penetrating gaze on truth. Experientially I know that lovingly giving myself to life creates a closeness of heart to everything.

Consider a small seashell—as I hold it in my hand and gaze upon it, I see more than just the mere seashell. I really see the seashell . . . the very fine lines that are marked upon it . . . I can feel the hardness of it . . . I can marvel at the creation of something so unique. There is not another in the whole world exactly like it; no other has served as the habitation of exactly the same specimen of life. I can ponder the God who allows such reality to be. I see the purple hue fade into the delicate ivory white on the edges, delicate lines still so present even now in this abandoned shell. For me, this shell becomes like no other shell.

I am present to its reality in much the same way that John Moffitt describes presence in this poem:

TO LOOK AT ANYTHING

To look at anything,
If you would know that thing,

You must look at it long;
To look at this green and say
'I have seen spring in these woods!'
will not do—you must
Be the thing you see,
You must be the dark snakes of stems
And ferny plumes of leaves,
You must enter in
To the small silence between.
You must take your time
And touch the very peace
They issue from.

Yes, we touch the very peace—Him from whom we all issue when we are present to reality whether this reality be a person, or nature, or a thing. Presence to seashells and leaves may seem insignificant when compared to presence to persons but unless we are present to rocks and trees, we will never learn to love a person. So it is possible to journey inwards and be free without the crises of suffering; however, our natural inclination is to avoid such deeper living. The next two chapters consider some of the reasons why.

PART II

SELF-ALIENATION—PSEUDO ESCAPE FROM SUFFERING

"I . . ."

CHAPTER II

PSYCHOLOGICAL ALIENATION

CONTEMPORARY SEARCH FOR AWARENESS

Have we grown so accustomed to the world that we miss it altogether? True, we cannot use all of our potential but, nevertheless, do we not often slide into a non-feeling, non-seeing, non-appreciative existence? Perhaps we are alienated from our real selves and thus unconsciously suppress inner dynamism. Or perhaps, we sometimes become so obsessed with life that we idolize any outward pull that makes us merely feel "alive".

John Gardner in his book, *Self Renewal,* proposes the diversion of travel as one means of awakening deadened senses.[1] R.D. Laing with tongue in cheek, advises a schizophrenic trip.[2] Some suggest that we use drugs to discover the unexplored areas of the self. Others advocate that we devote specific periods of time to transcendental meditation or yoga. We may have tried some of these means to break out of our encapsulated egos, yet isn't it true that most of our lives are lived in the ordinary? This very ordinariness, however, is filled with life and the "everyday" often reveals the extraordinary.

For example, You—I—can recall numerous rather

simple happenings. It is a balmy day and I can hear the birds. Suddenly in front of me I spy a crocus, the first one of spring. Unexpectedly the delicate flower lifts my spirit. It heralds the end of the cold gray winter months. In that leisurely moment of heightened awareness, its surprise beauty carries me somewhat out of myself.

At another time, hearing about the cardiac arrest of a mother of ten, I put aside my work and spend fearful waiting hours with the family. Sensing their genuine concern for their mother and for each other, I experience the intense unity of those who love, as well as the helplessness of those who wait. Had I rigidly followed the day's plans, life could not have surprised me with such feeling, painful as the circumstance was. In such intense involvement with life, commitment is both evoked and demanded and indeed the extraordinary, deep within the kernel of the ordinary is experienced.

POSSIBLE REASONS FOR LACK OF VITALITY

Perhaps though, we are too busy or so accustomed to the commonplace that we do not see everything every day as if for the first time. As a consequence, we may be out of tune with daily living and then wonder why life is dull and why we refuse real commitment and have little conviction about life values. While we search for some "ideal" world, the "real" world escapes us. We are unable to integrate special life experiences such as the moment of seeing the crocus as if for the first time, with the "space" between these experiences. Because we lack simplicity and singlemindedness we cannot experience ourselves as meaningfully whole.

Some say that Cartesian dualism is to blame for our

dichotomized approach to living. Present-day education and upbringing, unconsciously geared to "disinspirit" the child, seems to promote such duality. Classrooms often face drab buildings or parking lots or even in some instances are windowless e.g. in a school in Colorado Springs, awesome mountains were architecturally ignored by placing the windows facing brick walls and billboards. Even children can quickly forget about the surprise and delight of life by tedious repetitious study of mathematical abstractions, or by excessive emphasis on the correct way to print, write a poem or walk in an orderly line. Man can be programmed not to be a self, not to live his experiences, but rather to merely respond to social and cultural stimuli.

Could it be that we must search for ways to come alive, to be created because we have repressed reality, particularly when it is unpleasant? Money, time, and some of the best minds are devoted to man's collective attempt to conquer disease. Now that tuberculosis, smallpox, and polio threaten less, new diseases have come to our notice. Presently we are engaged in what seems to be, at last, a winning battle against heart disease and cancer. Our frenzied efforts to alleviate diseases of the body are partially successful because, in general, these diseases have been controlled. One wonders, however, if these physiological diseases are being replaced by an inner spiritual sickness of meaninglessness, alienation and fragmentation. Could such anguish be merely a distorted manifestation of the same basic disorder that was the basis of physical illness?

Perhaps our refusal to live unpleasant reality has conditioned us to build our lives on a fabric of falsehood. We may try to escape suffering through defensive behavior. Karen Horney, a German-American psychiatrist, discusses how defenses, may subtly poison our lives and may be the source of unnecessary suffering. In order to be freed of throttling defenses, it is essential that we recognize their presence. The fact that we face our defenses does not necessarily mean that we will change but unless we do face them, there is little possibility that we will grow beyond or through them.[3] Ordinarily, the best way out is through.

KAREN HORNEY'S THEORY AS IT RELATES TO ALIENATION

Karen Horney[4] contends that under favorable conditions our energies are directed to realizing our potential. Our very nature moves us to strive toward self-realization. However, under inner stress or suffering we may be alienated from our real selves and throw our energy into building a false, idealized self. This idealized self is based on a pride which is filled with doubts and self hate. To relieve the tension of this inner conflict we often assume attitudes of domination, self-effacement, or resignation.

Search for Glory and Idealized Self. It is important to see the difference between the neurotic search for glory and healthy human strivings because such distinction highlights how in searching for glory, a person often creates his own suffering. First, a neurotic personality is not able to be flexible. This means that he is unable to adapt to a given moment or to react differently to different situations. Second, the neurotic individual, in spite of favorable external possibilities, remains unproductive, since he feels that he stands in his own way.

This latter symptom, the inability to realize his potential, is at the root of the neurotic's rigid unrealistic image of himself. His energies are spent trying to keep intact a self-esteem which he considers ideal, but which is not in accord with his real potential. When he falls short of his idealized self, he blames his failure on external factors. He sets to work to mold himself into a supreme being of his own making. He holds before his soul an image of perfection and unconsciously tells himself: "Forget about the disgraceful creature you actually ARE; this is how you SHOULD be and to be this idealized self is all that matters."

Horney calls this the tyranny of the "shoulds." One should be able to endure everything, to like everybody, to understand everything, to be always productive. The neurotic has a need to be right and hence feels he should never be criticized, doubted or questioned. Because as a human person he is criticized, doubted and questioned he is doomed to suffer from the start, inauthentic though the suffering may be.

Self-Hate and Self-Contempt. When an individual shifts the center of his unique self to his idealized self, he exalts himself and must also look at his actual self from a distorted perspective. The glorified self is a phantom to be pursued as well as a measuring rod by which to judge his actual being. This actual being is such an embarassing sight when viewed from the perspective of godlike perfection that he cannot but despise it. His conflict ends in self hatred.

Self-hate indicates a rift in the personality which began with the creation of an idealized self. The person is not able to love himself. Such self-hate signifies that a war is on. Man, in reaching out for the Infinite and Absolute, also starts destroying himself. By his self idealization he figuratively makes a pact with the devil who promises him glory. In the process, he also has to go to hell, the hell within himself.

Three Major Neurotic Solutions.

In all these neurotic conflicts, the alienation from self is the core problem; in all of them we find the search for glory, the "shoulds" and the self-hate. How these factors operate in a particular neurotic structure depends upon the kind of solution the individual finds for his conflicts Horney distinguishes three major solutions: the expansive solution, the self-effacing solution and resignation. Each of these are ways to avoid authentic suffering and hence must be considered here.

Expansive Solution or Domination. In the expansive solution the individual usually identifies himself with his glorified self. The feeling of superiority that goes with this solution is not necessarily conscious but, nevertheless, it largely determines behavior, strivings and attitudes toward life in general. Life's fascination lies in its mastery. He should be able to master the adversities of fate, the difficulties of a situation, the resistances of other people and conflicts in himself. His most poignant dread is the dread of anything connoting helplessness. He tries to achieve mastery in different ways: by self admiration and the exercise of charm; by forcing fate through his demanding and high standards; by being invincible and conquering life in the spirit of revengeful triumph.

Self-effacing Solution; the Appeal of Love and Dependency. The second major solution of inner conflicts is the self-effacing solution. It moves in a direction which is essentially opposite to that of the expansive solution. He must not feel consciously superior to others or display any such feelings in his behavior. He tends to subordinate himself to others, to be dependent on them and to appease them. He cultivates and exaggerates his helplessness and suffering. He does not really want to suffer but abandoning himself to excessive suffering serves as an opiate against pain. Since admiration and recognition makes him uneasy he relinquishes the self through suffering. He longs for help, protection, and surrendering love. He lives with a sense of failure and hence tends to feel guilty, inferior or contemptible. He is his subdued self with no rights. He has solved his inner conflict by suppressing all expansive attitudes and drives.

His vindictive drives remain unconscious and can only be expressed indirectly. He is the underdog and identifies himself readily with others who are down trodden. The most characteristic way of expressing vindictive resentment is through suffering. Suffering also provides him with an overall alibi both for not making more of his life and for not achieving his goals.

Resignation. The third major solution to intrapsychic conflicts is withdrawal. Maintaining an attitude of "don't care," the neurotic feels less bothered by his inner conflicts and can attain a semblance of inner peace. He resigns from active living. Resignation, as used here, means settling for a peace which is merely the absence of conflicts. He is an onlooker at himself. He does not seriously strive for achievements and in fact has a real aversion for effort. He minimizes his assets and lacks goal direction. Though he does not mind observing things in himself, he does mind changing. His two outstanding neurotic claims are that life should be easy, painless and effortless and that he should not be bothered.

REFLECTIONS ON KAREN HORNEY'S THEORY

Though most of us do not have full-blown neuroses, each person has neurotic tendencies. Under stress, which is often a suffering experience, we may opt unconsciously for the avenues of domination, dependency, or resignation. As we become aware of our choices we may be free to grow beyond their clutch. A neurosis is generated not only by individual experience but also by the specific cultural conditions under which we live. The cultural conditions determine the final form of neurosis.

Idealized Self and Alienation. In subtle ways, we culturally learn the importance of being perfect, of being an "ideal self." As we page through the daily magazines, the ads frequently feature the perfectly built man and the beautifully sexy woman. Though it would seem that these "establishment" figures are rejected by many, at another level of consciousness they are often standards for comparison. We pick up this season's catalogs and find models are always chic and good looking. We assume that being fatter than these, being bald, or having crooked teeth is objectionable. Somehow we must strive to be perfect, to be, as Horney states, the idealized self. We cannot accept that we are limited, that we are not perfect. We should be perfect. Being perfect, we should not have to suffer.

We also learn ways to cope with stress from our parents and from those in society about us. In fact, we are very much what our parents were. As a child we learned from them what it was to be a man or a woman. Perhaps, more than we realize, we have assumed their way of handling stress. This may be a healthy way or it may be one in which we repress the reality of suffering. If we refuse the reality of suffering, we will have to deny experience. Temporarily, we may thus escape pain.

When we fail to become the idealized self that we have decided we should be, we blame external factors. This is somewhat exemplified in both of the following incidents taken from two different life forms.

Sister Aimee states:

> I came to religious life because I felt I could do in community what I could not do as an individual. Yet, year after year, I live with people with whom I cannot communicate. We have so little in common. With the structure of religious life being what it is, what hope is there for the accomplishment of depth communication and the achievement of common goals? I am not doing in community what I thought I could. I do not find the support and aid I came for. My efforts seem in vain.[5]

An exerpt from a friend's letter reads:

> I don't know what has happened to our marriage. We do not communicate. He has two jobs so the very structure of our lives does not allow us much time to be together, and now he must go to California for the summer, and I'll be left alone with three children. What is wrong? Why am I not finding what I expected in marriage?

The parallel between these two situations is obvious. It would seem that expectations of religious life, of marriage or perhaps of life itself are somewhat unrealistic. It may be that we are seeking an "ideal world" which is found only in fantasy and not in life as it is.

Solutions to Stress.

Horney presents three options typically chosen in the face of difficulties, none of which is clear cut and frequently two or three follow upon or are interwoven in a single individual's solution to stress. Such conflicting reactions can tear us apart psychologically. By resorting to conflicting defensive behavior in the face of suffering, we often experience a more frustrating and inauthentic suffering.

As stated previously, the common solutions to stress are the expansive solution or domination; the self-effacing solution or dependency; and the attitude of resignation. To clarify these further, an example of suffering is here presented and the three typical solutions we may use to avoid this stress follow. Let us note how this experience, though a source of suffering, is complicated and made more painful by refusal to accept human limitation. This specific individual, however, seems to be governed by an idealized self that demands nothing less than perfection and does not allow the recognition of unpleasant reality as a part of his life.

An Experience

Let's suppose that today is the local community fair. You—I—are the one in charge. As I back the car into the street, I dent the fender of my neighbor's Oldsmobile. It is my first accident. Later, enroute to the fair, I skid and scrape against the bridge railings scratching the right side of the car.

How this series of events is experienced is dependent on my attitude and approach to them. Perhaps one type of personality is more prone to have two accidents in succession than another, but here, bracket that possibility and merely consider how all three conflict solutions can enter into the way I live this situation. If my pattern of behavior follows that of mastery or the expansive solution, my reaction in such a situation may begin somewhat like this.

Last night I did not sleep very well. In fact, I woke

several times and always remembered today's responsibilities. This morning my stomach is upset. I know it is because I am very concerned about my part in the day's events. I am afraid that I will fail and I wish the day were over. Being nervous, I back into the street and dent my neighbor's car. I really do not understand how it happened. I have never had an accident before. I wonder if the whole day will go like this. Maybe I cannot assume responsibility for the fair. After talking with my neighbor, I decide not to tell my family since they might be concerned about me. Such is the way I rationalized my motive. The deeper truth may be that I do not want them to know I can fail.

I take a tranquilizer and try to relax. Enroute to the fair, I skid and scrape the car against a bridge railing which scratches the right side.

Arriving at the fair grounds, I decide to get hold of myself. Today must work out well. I direct those concerned in a dictatorial manner. This, at least, makes me appear confident, or so I think. I make contradictory demands on those who are helping me and others become irritated with me.

Realizing that my dominating behavior is ineffective, I initiate a change to the self-effacing position. I attempt to manipulate the others by arousing sympathy in them. I casually announce that I have had two accidents today. Nevertheless, I assure them that they really do not bother me. Later, however, I break into uncontrollable tears and blame everyone else for the day's difficulties. "If they would have done what I said; if others would have taken charge; they should have known how upset the accidents made me." I cannot confront them directly so I complain to those who are not involved, but who will sympathize with me and give me love.

At some point I may take the position of resignation. I decide that this event is over and that there is nothing I can do to change it. One thing I will do in the future, however, is never to become involved again. I will withdraw and not risk a similar occurrence. Repeatedly, I profess that I really "don't care."

In this experience, we use all three neurotic solutions and thus real conflict ensues. If at any point we are able to realistically accept the situation, our conflict lessens. When we can see that our failures, the car accidents, are indeed unfortunate but not necessarily the sign that we are worthless, that we cannot drive, that we can do nothing right, then we can move somewhat calmly to the next moments of our day. Unreasonably blaming ourselves for simple human error seems to indicate that to be human is not allowed. We must be perfect, we must indeed be godlike.

As we recognize and accept these behavior patterns in ourselves, we are already loosening their control over us. We see that we are mortal like everyone else, distressed and suffering from difficulties which we must outgrow.

These idealized demands that we place on ourselves do reflect the cultural milieu of which we are a part. In this chapter frequent references have been made to the influence of culture on our psychological attitude toward suffering. In the next chapter we focus specifically on the cultural aspect of alienation in today's society evidenced in loss of self and its accompanying anxiety. Such alienation is often the basis of inauthentic, unfruitful and unnecessary suffering.

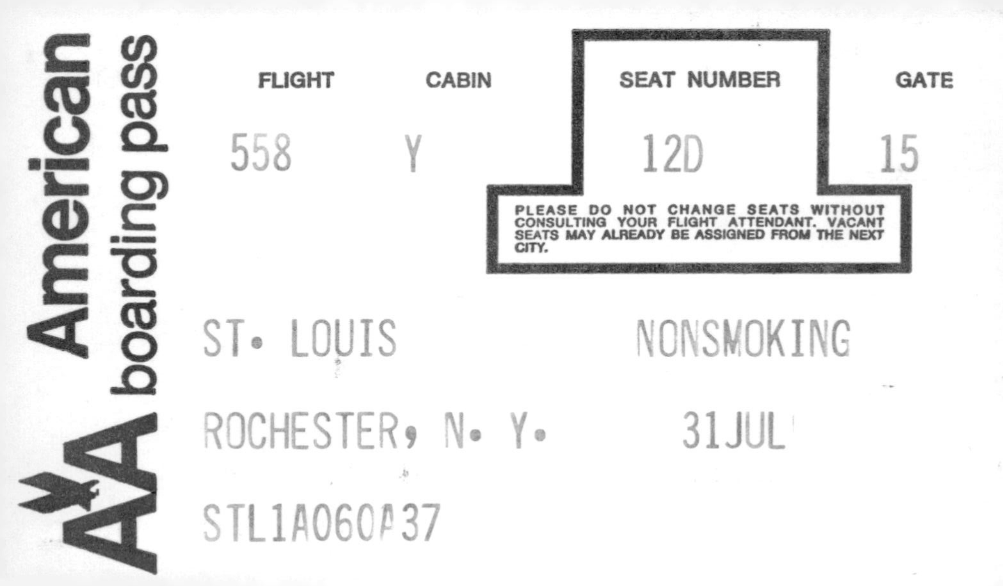
American
boarding pass
FLIGHT
558
CABIN
Y
SEAT NUMBER
12D
GATE
15
PLEASE DO NOT CHANGE SEATS WITHOUT CONSULTING YOUR FLIGHT ATTENDANT. VACANT SEATS MAY ALREADY BE ASSIGNED FROM THE NEXT CITY.
ST. LOUIS
NONSMOKING
ROCHESTER, N. Y.
31JUL
STL1A060A37

CHAPTER III

CULTURAL ALIENATION

Our alienation is all-pervasive. It influences our relationship to our work, to nature, to each other, to ourselves and to God. In current terms, "alienation" has been used to refer to a variety of psychosocial disorders including loss of selfhood, anxiety states, anomie, despair, depersonalization, apathy, loneliness, meaninglessness and the loss of beliefs or values. Whatever the approach, central to the definition of alienation is the idea that we have lost our identity or selfhood. This loss of self[1] with its concomitant anxiety is what specifically concerns us here.

Loss of Self

The loss of self is a certain abdication of our feelings, wishes and beliefs in the face of subtle levelling or conformism imposed by the "public". Because we fear ridicule if we are different from the crowd, we renounce our true desires and live as "they" dictate. This isolates us in the deepest sense from ourselves. We are as David Riesman says, lonely members of a lonely crowd busy "having fun."[2]

This crowd mentality hinders and stifles all initiative. Overenthusiasm for "equality" has *falsely* led to the belief that we are equal in all things. Naturally, this pseudo-equality necessitates reducing everyone to the same level.

When we interpret "equality" to mean "sameness" we are in trouble. To treat another equally is to treat the person according to his or her own unique needs, but not necessarily to treat him the same as another. For example, if we have twin children, a boy and a girl, we may give our son a birthday cake decorated like a basketball court because basketball is his favorite sport but our daughter may prefer a cake with petite horses and other equestrian decorations. This is to treat them, not the same, but uniquely or, as some would say, equally.

In the novel, *Eighth Day,*[3] Thornton Wilder shows how the "mass" demands that no one be different. In Coalton, which could be anywhere, Lansing, who symbolizes evil, is a jolly regular guy, proudly the center of everything. Ashley, who is falsely convicted of murdering Lansing, is an unassuming, integrated individual who, in contrast to Lansing, cannot even create a real stir at his trial. His very composure and "at homeness" in existence only arouses curiosity. Had Lansing killed Ashley, Wilder declares, Lansing would have been cowed and frightened and then acquitted. Not so Ashley. Without excuse or fanfare he dares to live his convictions, and though innocent, he is, nevertheless, condemned. At the cost of much suffering, Ashley does rise above the levelling process. He is true to what is most genuinely himself and thus orders his life rather than permit his life to order him. At least temporarily, he escapes the levelling process and the loss of self.

Loneliness Anxiety

On the other hand, submitting to the "levelling process" initiates its own kind of suffering, namely, alienation and its accompanying effects such as the loss of self. The loneliness which characterizes this loss of self is described by Clark Moustakas as a form of loneliness anxiety and is not to be confused with existential loneliness, which is an inevitable but real and healthy loneliness.

In existential loneliness we are fully aware of ourselves as isolated and solitary individuals while in loneliness anxiety we are separated from ourselves as feeling and knowing persons. This loneliness anxiety results from a breach between what we are and what we pretend to be. We no longer have an intimate sense of relatedness to our world. Separated from direct and personal contact with creation, we are starving for communion with other persons and with all aspects of life and nature. This loneliness anxiety is manifested in a form of bland existence which stifles self emergence and self realization.[4]

Such loneliness appears to be accentuated in our industrial-urban society by movements which reject family unity; by fewer intimate associations with neighbors; by general wariness of criminal assault; by a functionary attitude toward people; and by high mobility, all of which seem to have a disintegrating effect upon us.

We are isolated from each other, and even though we meet many people there is little intimacy. Such intimacy is only possible when we know ourselves. To come to this self awareness, a degree of solitude and aloneness is necessary. However, interiority may not be lived because present crowded environments seldom provide moments or places for meaningful distance. Neither does the modern day milieu foster an appreciation for the values interiority may promote. Desmond Morris compares civilized man with the captive animals confined in the unnatural conditions of a zoo. There, an animal, ostracized from its natural habitat, will mutilate itself, masturbate, attack its offspring, develop stomach ulcers and suffer from obesity. In a similar manner, the urban man caged in crowded cities may exhibit neurotic behavior patterns.[5]

Societal Evidences of Alienation

There are multiple examples of man's inhumanity to man, which evidence alienation from that which is life giving. Randomly selecting a few authors who have addressed themselves to this deplorable inhumanity, we mention John Howard Griffin who shows the enormous wall of hostility between the black and the white race.[6] Benjamin Epstein and Arnold Foster who cite specific cases of Anti-Semitism operating in education, employment and housing;[7] John Grimes, a psychiatrist, who tells about the sadistic violence with which the mentally ill are treated and the political system which gives jobs to brutal and unqualified attendants;[8] Edgar May who presents a candid insight into the welfare program and highlights the loneliness and boredom of the old and unemployed.[9]

These and other examples highlight our alienation. When we lose touch with ourselves, we no longer love and respect the self that we are nor the uniqueness of others. Life is not lived but life is merely something to be lived through.

Examples of an Alienated Individual

In the novel, *A Burnt Out Case,* Graham Greene presents Querry, his hero, as cut off from nearly every human feeling, and hence Querry is bored and unable to suffer or to experience joy.

Querry expresses his feelings of alienation and boredom in several exchanges. In dialogue with the superior of the religious community, Querry declares at one point, ". . . I suffer from nothing. I no longer know what suffering is."[10] One night in telling a story to Mme. Rycker, he seems to be describing himself when he relates,

> . . . The only trouble was that he became bored, more and more bored. Nobody ever made him suffer—it was always the other people who suffered. Sometimes just for a change he would have welcomed feeling the pain of the punishment.[11]

His inability to feel is an all-pervasive one. Discussing his inability to love and wondering if he has ever loved, he begins to question whether he has deceived himself with work as well. However, he has not killed all feeling in himself or, at least, feeling begins to be reawakened upon reading a letter of anguish from Mme. Rycker. It occurs to him that one can be sensitive to the reflection of another's pain even when one has ceased to feel one's own.

Querry seems to know he is out of touch with his feelings and this initiates a return to himself. Dr. Colin further prods Querry by asking him whether he wouldn't rather suffer than feel discomfort, alleging that discomfort irritates our ego like a mosquito bite, and that sometimes the search for suffering and the remembrance of suffering are the only means we have to put ourselves in touch with the human condition. To this Querry requests, "Then I wish you'd teach me how to suffer. I only know the mosquito bites."[12]

However, his boredom perdures. Even in the final chapter, Deo Gratias, his cured leper servant, wonders why Querry could not go back to where he came from and sounds out Querry, "Have you killed a man?" To this Querry retorts, "I have killed everything."[13]

Querry later finds that he does suffer from the false and grave accusations of the envious Rycker, and remarks, "I thought I had become incapable of feeling pain."[14] Because he befriends Mme. Rycker and also confronts her husband, both indications of his emerging selfhood, Querry is murdered by Rycker.

Daring to live authentically costs Querry his life and yet seems to have been his happiness, as well. Querry, shortly before his death admits this truth to Colin, "I think I'm cured of pretty well everything, even disgust. I've been happy here."[15]

Personal Experience of Cultural Alienation

Like Querry, we too, are influenced by cultural alienation. At one time in my own life I considered reflection on suffering somewhat morbid. It seemed to me that there was enough pain in the world without my thinking about it. Unfeelingly I pretended that suffering was merely to be expected and somewhat disregarded and then perhaps it would cease to exist. Because I did not often listen to or experience my own suffering, I found it difficult to be genuinely compassionate toward others who suffered. In fact, I tried to make my life meaningful by concentrating on joy. Hence, I read books about joy and in some project-like fashion tried to bring joy to others.

Now, having spent several years reading, writing and thinking about this long avoided subject, I have discovered a wider awareness of suffering's mystery and value by having wrestled with it. Paradoxically, I am now more joyful. I need not listen in a mere "counselor" fashion to other's accounts of suffering but can more genuinely understand them since I also admit the experience of the burdensome, the awkward and the painful.

Dialogue Between Originality and Suffering

Living suffering also evokes our originality. Suffering throws us back on ourselves and when we allow it to enter our lives it shows us that we are limited. In this reflective distance we gradually accept and come to the truth of ourselves.[16] Authentic suffering, because of the inwardness it fosters, thus promotes the unveiling of our originating selves and new dimensions of the person are revealed. We find an inward center of gravity. When absent from true selfhood and interiority, we do not genuinely experience suffering. Instead we live in an unreality that is at times people with pseudo-fantasized conflicts or with no recognition of conflict at all. It is at these moments that we are unwilling to be who we are. In diverse ways we escape from that authentic suffering which, in showing us our insufficiency, could further both our purification and the emergence of our own originality or selfhood. We escape the suffering that could give visible embodiment to our inner spiritual universe.

Originality and suffering are in dialogue. As we live from our unique center we experience sufferings authentically and the more authentically we live our sufferings, the more our selfness is called forth. Although a lack of selfhood is frequently a barrier to authentic suffering and characterizes an alienated and escapist life, we would be mistaken if we merely waited for our originality to emerge before we embraced life's suffering. Rather, it is by falteringly living with ambiguity that we continually risk discovering, both authentically and inauthentically, "who we are." By willingly being "on the way" we realize that we will always be arriving.[17] Through a patient and humble dialogue with all that is a part of our lives, we may slowly come to know the real. Then, gradually we may let go of that which threatens and shackles the emergence and revelation of our true selves.

In conclusion, let us emphasize that willingness to take risks often indicates the degree to which we are alive. Of course, these risks cannot be a form of despair or suicide but rather the risks of courageous dynamic living which touch the wonder of life at its roots. In Part III we will consider some of the positive values that suffering can foster in our lives.

PART III

BECOMING A PERSON THROUGH AUTHENTIC RESPONSE TO SUFFERING

". . . finally learned . . ."

CHAPTER IV

SUFFERING AS WARNING

> Suffering in itself is not evil. Like happiness, it is an experience which turns to good or evil according to the way we live it.
>
> —E. Cammaerts

In examining life, we find that suffering has exercised a great influence on us. Suffering has given us a certain seriousness and depth. From suffering we draw fundamental lessons about the world in which we are called to live and about ourselves and the meaning of our lives.

Suffering is indeed a laceration, a division of self against self, a conflict and even a rupture of our inner person. We suffer but do not want to suffer and hence we experience disunity within. It is precisely this that makes us ask if suffering is really a "privation of being." In suffering there is an injury or wound that affects us, hence in this sense there seems to be a privation of being. Suffering does, however, give to our consciousness an extraordinary awareness in which we may question the meaning of suffering and the meaning of life itself.

When we ask what positive meaning suffering can have for us or what meaning our will can give it, we notice that it can be for us either a warning, a condition of refinement and depth, a means of communion with others or, finally, an instrument of interior purification.[2]

SUFFERING AS WARNING

Suffering is a warning when it is an indication of a threatening danger. In the form of pain it moves the bodily organism to avoid dangerous stimuli to body tissue. Psychologically, suffering invites even the most superficial to reflect. It warns against what Viktor Frankl calls psychic death, since suffering provides the tension necessary to help us keep our goal in focus and thus lead a meaningful life.[3]

The Tension of Suffering as Warning

Frankl[4] states that when we suffer, there is a tension between "what is" and "what ought to be."[5] So long as the tension prevails we suffer. This suffering warns us that all is not as it should be. For example, when a loved husband is ill, his wife also suffers because she experiences tension between what is, her husband's sickness, and what she considers ought to be, namely, his healthy well-being. If she were indifferent to her husband, she would not experience this tension.

Tension Accompanies Meaning

Frankl maintains that our search for meaning and values causes inner tension rather than inner equilibrium. In this search we find gaps between what we are and what we hope to become.[6] The resulting tension is inherent in a human being and is indispensable to mental and creative well-being.[7]

Frankl's theory of logotherapy focuses on our search for meaning. Logotherapy attempts to move us from self-centeredness to a fuller awareness of life. It is in this awareness of life and the subsequent awareness of life's demands that meaning is discovered. A selfish wife would not be concerned about her husband's well-being. She would not help him recover. According to Frankl, it is in working toward this goal, in this case, good health, that meaning is found.

Lack of meaning in life seems to be a common phenomenon. This boredom and meaninglessness is often escaped by engrossing ourselves in a whirlwind of activities and a work-world of efficiency. Frankl presents two reasons for this meaninglessness or existential vacuum, as he terms it.[8]

Reasons For Meaninglessness

The first of these reasons is the rapid breakdown of tradition which has alienated us from ourselves. To deny the part tradition plays in life is to be out of touch with reality. Such uprootedness can be tolerated when we are divorced from our past and live in a purely mechanical way. Not knowing what we wish to do, we do instead what we think others expect of us. Such conformity eventually becomes boring.

Indeed, we live in a culture in which the collective neurosis is boredom or what Frankl calls "noogenic" neurosis. This very boredom, however, can be the suffering which leads to a new awareness of life and meaning. If we face the boredom which confronts us with questions, we may unveil meaning. If, however, we repress boredom by frantically pursuing money or pleasure, e.g. by working at two or even three jobs or by continually being "on the go" we deaden our feelings and increase our frustration.

Besides the rapid breakdown in tradition, impersonal technology also fosters a nihilistic approach to life. Scientism tends to manipulate us as things. Ideals and values, since they cannot be measured mathematically, have no place in a merely technological world.

Suffering Can Impel Me to Look for Meaning

Suffering, provided it is not escaped, can impel us to look deeper within ourselves for meaning. We must not, however, expect to discover an abstract, final, universal meaning. We each discover our own specific and unique meaning. It may vary from hour to hour and from task to task. True meaning is found in the world, not in our psyche. We do not invent meaning; we detect it. Meaning is that which pulls us to responsibility and commitment. It cannot be taught or given; we can only live it. Meaning challenges rather than drives us to moral and responsible behavior. For example, because we regard life as a meaningful gift, high in our hierarchy of values, we will be eager to preserve life in all its forms. This may be evidenced as we become knowledgeable in the area of ecology. When we understand the destructive nature of pollutants, anti-pollution laws will not be essential to insure our ethical response to preserve that which is life giving.[9]

Our meaning or goal is not directly self-actualization or even happiness. Rather, meaningful fulfillment of self is an effect of honest self-transcendence. This means that fulfillment is found by looking away from success and happiness, and by reaching out beyond ourselves through commitment to a cause. A lack of success does not imply a lack of meaning because there can be meaning in failure.

In speaking with boys who have returned from the anguish of Vietnam or with missionaries who have identified with the Africans or Brazilians or with those who labor with the migrant families, we realize how these dedicated individuals frequently involve and risk themselves beyond what is ordinarily expected. In this very transcendence they discover a new sense of life. These difficult situations become opportunities to actualize attitudinal values, and life is experienced as being lived rather than lived through. With Frankl we can affirm that personal fulfillment is found not by concentrating on self-realization but by honest involvement with life and its demands.

Our attitudes influence how we live and particularly how we suffer. If our attitude is healthy, suffering becomes something more than that which we egotistically hug to ourselves or that which crushes us. Suffering is something deeper than a self-centered experience of agony. When we experience suffering in this detached way, we are not freed from suffering but we may realize the deeper meaning to which suffering points. We can, then, through suffering actualize value potentials that enrich our lives. We find that life is fulfilled not only by productivity and enjoyment but by creative suffering as well.

For example, suffering makes us conscious of our finite and limited nature. It helps us to step back from life and again see and accept both ourselves and reality as it is. We learn again that all is on loan, all is gift and that we are not the owner or controller of life. Rather we are the gifted recipients of countless benefits and only in the stance of gratitude are we true to the nature that is basically ours.

There are times when we can fulfill ourselves only in

genuine suffering. It is true that, in a given situation, we may be unable to remove suffering; however, we are not necessarily predetermined. We can be self-determined by the decisions we make in regard to adversity. In the following example we can see the contrast between the passive psychic death of hopelessness and maintaining life through the tension of striving.

Two persons are in the same ward of the hospital; each is suffering from a similar crippling illness. One of them regards her illness with despair and will probably never leave her bed again; the second is now learning to walk and plans to teach school this next term. Rather than being predetermined by her suffering and passively abandoning herself to fate, the latter person takes a stand in regard to it and this leads to her partial recovery.

To the degree that we identify with things as they are, we eliminate the fruitful tension between what is and what healthily ought to be.[10] We also eliminate the possibility of creativity and growth. By the diversion of drugs or alcohol, we can take our minds off what happens, but in doing so, we escape reality and do not grow or come to terms with our particular misfortune. In fact, we become oblivious to it. Consistently suppressing emotional impulses because of their unpleasantness kills inner life. Suffering has value in preserving vitality because, if accepted, it can guard us from psychic *rigor mortis* or apathy. In a similar vein, Spinoza says that as soon as we cease to suffer, we cease also to be.[11]

Like death, sorrow and trouble are a part of life. Through suffering, life gains shape and form. However, we should not too quickly accept that which may be merely imaginary fate. Only when we have no possibility of modifying or changing a situation is it time for attitudinal values; then alone should we "take up our cross" and experience the deepest possible meaning.

Life is a constant opportunity waiting for actualization. If we are willing to experience the tension of the painful, suffering can bring us to truth. Through reflection on suffering our purposes and goals in life are often re-examined and purified of the unwholesomeness that quickly taints a complacent life. We may return to our inner selves and be made whole once again through the hurt of a misunderstanding that leads us to examine our motives or the anguish of a rejection that makes us realize what is ultimate. Continually, the ongoing rhythm of life's suffering reminds us that we have not yet arrived.

We also learn that suffering is a mystery. We experience this, not as a matter of thinking, but rather as a matter of believing. We catch hold of this meaning not on intellectual ground but on existential ground; that is, through our whole being, through faith.

CHAPTER V

SUFFERING AS A CONDITIONING FOR REFINEMENT AND DEPTH

> Your joy is your sorrow unmasked . . . The deeper that sorrow carves into your being, the more joy you can contain.[1]

Besides warning us against bodily tissue damage or psychic death, suffering can also foster a certain refinement and depth within us. Louis Lavelle says suffering is not just an isolated state. We are whole and all of our interior states are interdependent. If we sacrifice one, we compromise the entire unity of our being. We value what we do because of the sufferings we have sustained as well as the joys we have been given. This unity within our being implies that the interior states of suffering and joy interpenetrate one another.[2]

Unity of Joy and Suffering

Sometimes joy is considered the opposite of suffering and yet the more we enter into our lives, the more both joy and suffering seem to merge. In one way sufferings are like the shadows that make it possible for us to appreciate and see the light.

As I write this, the sun is at its zenith, the white clouds lazily move across the pale blue sky. The trees where the sun strikes them are a lighter shade of green while the leaves in the shadows are darker green. If it were not for the shadows the sight before me would be a glaring one, one from which I would quickly avert my eyes.

Though my analogy is inadequate, experientially it would seem that in life, too, the light of joy is tempered by the dark of suffering. Paradoxical, as it is, joy and suffering are intimately interwoven. In joy we momentarily know the possibility of suffering. Contrariwise without the possibility of suffering we could not experience joy. At one time joy is figure and suffering is ground; at another suffering is figure and joy is ground. This means that when we experience joy, suffering recedes to the background. Nevertheless, both are present just as when we are with a friend, (figure) the surroundings (ground) are often oblivious to us. Hence, even though we may forget the possibility of suffering or only momentarily reflect that suffering can intrude on present joy, suffering is still latently present.

The Dutch psychiatrist, W.J.J. de Sauvage Nolting, expresses the opinion that though unhappiness may be the first experience of a living being, the possibility of experiencing happiness[3] is created at the same moment. He says that we know from experience that after a period of thirst the fact that we are at last satiated creates a feeling of comfort and even of happiness. He believes this happens because we think back and in contrast are still influenced by our previous thirst.

Human experience also teaches that happiness and comfort cannot last forever and this creates a feeling of uncertaintity which is a latent suffering. In striving for something, we, in one sense, always experience the thing striven for as already accomplished. In a contrary sense, the state of happiness creates a feeling of anxiousness. Even if this anxiousness lasts only for an infinitesimal part of a second, no living being can escape from it. Such knowledge seems to possess a hereditary base. Through ages of experience we "know". The "flash" need not be fully conscious. Generally speaking we try to suppress this remembrance or force it to the background. However, we never experience happiness without this perhaps subconscious knowledge of pain. To experience joy, a certain tension must remain, otherwise our happiness will be as Nolting says, "statical 'dead' happiness."[4]

Ladislaus Boros speaks of this joylessness which seems similar to Nolting's "statical dead happiness" as a sort of existential flatness.[5] He says that in such a state it is easy to live an uninvolved and unhappy life because it takes no effort. In joylessness, human life becomes universally livable. Nothing unique ever happens. Here we live in a world that may function well, but it is flat or uniformly grey. It is not that we experience difficult things and are weakened but rather our lives are all too easy. We don't think too much. We don't expect too much. We refuse to live the mystery that accompanies the tension of suffering and the "burden of joy." Our refusal, however, also condemns us to live as a joyless person in a world of uninterrupted banality.

Individuals who live through periods of great misery often create the most splendid works of art. Real art is born from a burning desire to achieve something better and nobler. The emotions portrayed by dramatists, sculptors and painters are unimaginable without suffering. For the artist as well as the contemplative, creating is a kind of catharsis. It is a way to let out bottled-up emotions. Through suffering, artists manifest latent creative mechanisms and attain joyful experiences.[6] Suffering does not create but it does bring into manifest existence "reaction forces" which would never have come into existence if they had not been born in suffering.[7]

Herman Hesse dramatizes this unity of suffering and joy and the sensitive creativity that the refinement of suffering can initiate in the novel, *Narcissus and Goldmund.* The story centers around two extraordinary persons, Brother Narcissus, a young handsome Greek teacher who, though loved by many, is at times resented by others for his extreme reserve and self control, and Goldmund, a delicate beautiful adolescent enrolled at the cloister school. Narcissus is an analytical thinker while Goldmund is a dreamer with the soul of a child. Both are refined and gifted, and each finds a complement in the other.

Narcissus, who reads people better than most, does not believe in Goldmund's calling to be an ascetic. In exchanges with Narcissus, Goldmund comes to realize that he, Goldmund, has forgotten his childhood, his past, his mother. As his eyes are opened to her, "He saw the tall, radiant woman with the full mouth and glowing hair—his mother."[8] He trembles with pain and joy. His father had instilled in Goldmund the conviction that he must offer his life to God to expiate his mother's sins and thus Goldmund, having been constantly reminded of the shame of his mother, forgot her real image. Meeting a young girl, Lise, he feels that his mother, whom he had venerated, admired and unconditionally loved, has come to take him home. Goldmund realizes that he has confused his father's orders with his own wishes. He takes leave of Narcissus and the cloister and begins his search for a goal.

One night, a peasant woman whose guest he is, gives birth to a child. He assists by holding the light and is awed to find that the lines in the screaming woman's distorted face are little different from those he has seen in other women's faces during the moment of love's ecstacy. Some time later, in his wanderings, he visits a church and is enthralled by the same phenomenon. This time it is a mysterious statue, ". . . in whose face so much pain and sweetness are living side by side that it made his heart ache."[9] He leaves the church possessing what he has so often mocked and envied in others: a goal.

He seeks out the artist carver and tells him of witnessing a birth in which he found that ". . . the greatest pain and the most intense ecstacy have almost the same expression."[10] He says, too, that he has found the same in this master's carved madonna, ". . . Oh, there is such suffering in the beautiful delicate face, and at the same time all the suffering is also pure joy, a smile. . . ."[11] Goldmund's goal is to make visible some day a figure that is not to represent any specific woman, but the source of life itself, the original mother. He wants it to show "the intimate relationship of ecstacy to pain and death."[12]

To Goldmund, the soaring blissful burning of desire for life seems to contain the kernel of all experience. It becomes to him an image of all the joys and sufferings of life. He can give in to this melancholy and shudder at all things transitory with the same abandonment with which he gives in to love. This melancholy is also a form of love. Death and ecstacy are one. The mother of life can be called love or desire; she can also be called death, grave or decay. Her image, which Goldmund carries within him, becomes a parable and a sacred symbol to him.

Sensitivity Heightened in Suffering

Each suffering of Goldmund's life makes him more sensitive. Physical suffering teaches him the presence of his body. Moral suffering gives him a certain seriousness. This is evidenced in his response to the plague. Upon visiting a house in the woods he discovers five corpses. Robert, his companion, takes a glimpse at one of them, screams and leaves wide-eyed with fright. Goldmund, however, sees the gruesomeness but also the nobility of the dead and slowly remarks upon leaving the place, "It was not terrible, I saw nothing in there that does not await you and me and everybody, even if we don't catch the plague."[13] One time later in life Goldmund remarks, "Pain? Yes, I have had pains enough. But you see, pains are not so bad; they've brought me to reason . . ."[14]

Values Stand in Relief

Through Goldmund's suffering his attachments to egocentric plans become more evident. In suffering, too, he becomes aware of what he values. As Goldmund enters the plague-stricken city, he is struck by the absence of the sound of life which formerly greeted him. Now, in this empty street nothing echoes, no one laughs, no one cries, everything lies frozen in deathly silence except the overloud running well. Goldmund sees a pretty girl and pleads with her to leave this city of death. "We'll go into the woods and live a good life."[15] Although he is stripped of what he has been, he does not despair or become suspicious of all persons and of life itself. Instead he turns his attention to what is and involves himself in an authentic personal relationship which brings him much joy. In truly experiencing through the plague what he has lost, he becomes aware, in meeting his beloved, of what he has gained. However, embracing her is an eventual embracing of grief, as well, since their relationship is later terminated by her awful death from the plague. This again echoes the truth that joy and sorrow seem to be the rhythm of real life.

Another time, after having completed a fine carving of St. John and being recommended to the guild by Master Niklaus, Goldmund is surprised to find that he is not happy. He roams about the city, watching the movement at the market place, feeling pity for the fish and a sad annoyance for human beings who so obliviously and cruelly kill these fish. He is plunged into solitude, contemplating suffering and death and the vanity of all undertaking. It would seem that his interior being is rendered fertile by a new awareness. In one sense, he is revealed to himself. In this moment of emptiness, he discovers that he yearns for more in life than success.

Goldmund is led back to the cloister where Narcissus is now the abbot. At Narcissus' invitation, he remains there and begins carving wood panels for the lectern in the refectory. In these carvings, he places the consciousness of life which the ebb and flow of suffering have given him. By assuming his sufferings rather than rejecting them or becoming enslaved to them he has made them into himself. He is not afraid to be conscious of his misery.

Suffering As a Condition for Growth

The worst misery is not to be aware of misery. When we become less concerned about ridding ourselves of suffering as Goldmund did and more concerned about repairing the insufficiency it symbolizes, then suffering becomes a condition for interior growth. We can never return to the state in which we were when suffering began. Consciousness cannot have, as an object of desire, a state through which it has already passed. Suffering has meaning when we are unable to tolerate it and thus are directed toward a state which transcends it. Such a state constitutes progress and not regress.

There is not a region in our inner life where suffering cannot some day penetrate. Every new acquisition, every new growth is the occasion of a new wound. In the interval between what we have and what we desire, the aptitude for suffering is found. Suffering is the other side of our power of transcendence.[16] In exercising our aptitude for suffering, we can also know the joy of transcendence.

Let us ponder more specifically some aspects of this truth. It is through *reflection* upon an evil, or an attachment, or a life experience that suffering is conceived or generated. If we did not have a memory, in most instances, we would not suffer. This reflection occurs in the unique solitude that we are. Our capacity for solitude and our capacity for suffering increase proportionately to each other. In solitude we are most ourselves and the more genuinely we experience and communicate with self, the more we are able to communicate with the solitude of others. In this discovery of "who we are" in communion with self and others, superficiality is cast aside and true joy is known.

CHAPTER VI

SUFFERING AS A MEANS OF COMMUNICATION WITH OTHERS

We suffer most from those we love; just as we experience the greatest joy with them. In one way we are imprisoned in solitude and yet, without a consciousness of separation, we cannot experience personal communion. That which is most ourselves also constitutes the obstacle against which our efforts to communicate flounder. What we want to penetrate in another is inpenetrable; what we want to give cannot be received. We find that we suffer from what separates us from others in proportion to our desire for union.[1] Nonetheless, Rollo May holds that "the essence of being human is that, in the brief moment we exist on this spinning planet, we can love some persons and some things in spite of the fact that time and death will ultimately claim us all."[2]

Multiple life experiences might be explored in discussing this relationship of love to suffering. Here, I limit my remarks to one of Bernard Malamud's short stories, "Magic Barrel," and show experientially how suffering can be an avenue for communion with another.

Morality for Malamud means responsibility and commitment. If one loves, one responds. The more genuine a person's love, the more he assumes responsibility and commits himself to the demands of love. In his writings Malamud frequently shows the self-centeredness and miserable routine existence of the loveless person. Through many interior and exterior experiences of anguish and pain, Malamud confronts this unhappy individual with the truth about himself. Consider how the protagonist in "Magic Barrel" learns to love through suffering.

"Magic Barrel"

Leo Finkle, a rabbinical student, is soon to be ordained and has been advised by an acquaintance that he might find it easier to win himself a congregation if he were married. Since Finkle has no prospects of marriage, he calls a marriage broker. The matchmaker, Salzman, presents him with a number of possibilities, all of whom Finkle rejects. After visiting Leo a second time, Salzman is able to arouse Finkle's curiosity about one prospect, Lily Hirschhorn. He goes walking with her, and her probing questions force him to reveal more truth about himself than he intends or, in fact, than he himself knows. In facing the reality about himself, Finkle comes to the shocking discovery

> . . . that he did not love God as well as he might, because he had not loved man. It seemed to Leo that his whole life stood starkly revealed and he saw himself for the first time as he truly was—unloved and loveless. This bitter but somehow not fully unexpected revelation brought him to a point of panic, controlled only by extraordinary effort. He covered his face with his hands and cried.[3]

Finkle's studies had led him to know the word but not the spirit. He now questions his whole life as well as his ministerial calling. In his remorse and distress he has no one to whom he may turn. With time, he does gain some composure and some idea of purpose in life and decides to continue in this ministry as planned. He realizes that he is imperfect but takes consolation in the hope that his ideal is not. He resolves to seek a bride without the help of a matchmaker and truly wants to love the one he marries.

On one of his visits Salzman has left a portfolio of pictures with Leo. For a long while Leo refuses to look at them; however, one lonely morning he tears open the packet. With excitement he studies the faces of the ladies, but he finds them uninspiring. Returning the photos to the envelope, he notices a cheap snapshot that he had previously missed. He gazes at it a moment and is overwhelmed. Frantically, he searches out Salzman to learn the girl's identity and is told that the photo was put there by accident. This girl is a wild one without shame and she is certainly not fit to wed a rabbi. Animatedly, Finkle presses Salzman for more information and the old man in a burst of tears says, "This is my baby, my Stella, she should burn in hell."[4]

Finkle rushes home. There he thinks through his life and faces the climactic test which will determine his future.

> Through days of torment he endlessly struggled not to love her; fearing success, he escaped it. He then concluded to convert her to goodness, himself to God. The idea alternately nauseated and exalted him.[5]

This ordeal prepares Leo for love and, despite Salzman's pleas to desist, a meeting is arranged. As Leo meets Stella and looks into her eyes, he knows, though Stella is a girl of the streets, that she is his redemption.

Leo has lived selfishly isolated from others and because of it, life passed him by. In surrendering to Stella he is freed from self-sufficiency and moral platitudes. Though Stella's life has not always been reputable, she has awakened "religious" Leo to his real self and thus saves him from his false, idealized self.

We, like Leo, are periodically shown the undesirable realities about ourselves. Refusal to face these truths stifles personality development. By denying reality we diminish awareness and try to eliminate suffering. On the other hand, being our real selves we dip into the universality of being and are in communion with all beings. Love then transforms us; we become creators rather than sufferers.

Often, however, our greatest suffering is that caused by our inability to relieve the sufferings of those we love. This standing-by or waiting is particularly difficult when we are separated from them. Until we can be near them and/or until we can at least be assured that their pain is less, our own anguish is unbearable. Our utter helplessness to change their life situation or to understand the mystery of their person fills us with indescribable loneliness, fear and sadness. Our awareness of our limitations is heightened in this suffering.

We discover, too, that deep within ourselves is a gentle, loving person.[4] The rationality of logical talk does not solve problems or meet needs. Compassion and love do.

However, without interiority so-called love may be merely an attempt to meet our own neediness. But with interiority we can grow in awareness of our motivation and thus be more genuinely loving. Tenderness is sensitive, affectionate, gentle and sympathetic. Man's capacity for fear and suspicion is almost without limit, so also his capacity to lap up tenderness is practically infinite.

In a recent Peanuts comic strip, Lucy is saying to Schroeder, "Do you think I'm the most beautiful girl in the world?" Naturally she has to ask several times in different ways until Schroeder, to be rid of her "botheration," says "Yes". Lucy mopes disconsolately, "Even when he says it, he doesn't say it." How often this is true in our lives. Our bodies speak so much louder than our hollow words that we often do not hear or accept the words that are spoken.

Hence, much depends on the way we extend tenderness. We all have a self protecting shield which is healthy. At one moment we bid another to enter and at the next we say, "Stay away." Through experience we gradually learn how best to be tender with each unique person. Also, in tenderness we acknowledge to our friend our vulnerability and fragility. Since this is a risk, it demands trust. Consequently, the double bind of bidding another to come in and yet to stay distant often operates.

Just yesterday I met a person with whom I hadn't communicated for about ten years. She was someone I had always enjoyed. I expressed this to her in front of another and her uncomfortableness was evidenced by the remark, "My, aren't we full of compliments today!" Momentarily, I felt that my affirmation of her was inappropriate.

In our Western culture, which has always emphasized our sinfulness, it is indeed difficult to accept, much less ponder, the affirmation of goodness that others give us. Such being the situation, it is also a bit scary to extend love because none of us likes to be rejected. Hence, fear and false morality may condemn us to loneliness.

However, loneliness and sometimes painful insights, if accepted, initiate further personality growth and can be the beginning of a more respectful presence to life and an even deeper love.

Pain can identify us with the afflictions of others and we thus unite with them in a more loving way. In an awareness of our miseries, the freed inner self may reach the heights of compassion and goodness. We may be on the way to achieving that humanity of heart which makes life meaningful.

CHAPTER VII

SUFFERING AS A MEANS OF PURIFICATION

All negative and positive aspects of suffering are mutually related; thus, this discussion of them may seem repetitious. However, in addition to the consciousness of our attachments, the aspect of purification treats the added dimension of cleansing and purgation that suffering may initiate. This purifying is closely related to the freeing of man's spirit. Hence, our observations here serve as a bridge into the next part which considers the religious nature of person and suffering.

When we willingly assume suffering, we acquire a delicacy and sensitivity. In some way we are purified of a certain carelessness toward ourselves and others. We become conscious of the incongruency between our professed beliefs and our actual lived values. When we become aware of our attachments to lesser values we are free to choose more ultimate values. Louis Lavelle's work regarding purification further elucidates these truths.

Purification Aspect As Presented by Louis Lavelle[1]

In previous reflections, suffering has been discussed as an avenue toward greater interiority. According to Lavelle, there has always been a close connection between purification and the deepening of self. Our instinctual life is governed by natural impulses and environmental influences. As our consciousness chooses to counteract these specific impulses and influences, we may possibly be enriched. On the other hand, our consciousness or reflective powers can also threaten our interior life and thus create a new peril for us.

For example, in all that we are attached to, there is that which belongs to us but which is not us, which makes us go out of ourselves and this, precisely is the source of vanity. If we seek from these objects outside of us a satisfaction of self-love or a means of distraction, then our personality dissolves rather than grows. What matters is not necessarily what we possess but rather our attitude toward what we have. This is true of both visible possessions and invisible ones such as knowledge, intelligence and virtue. The pleasure we draw from the latter is often a deeper and more subtle form of vanity. Abnegation or purification consists in turning our attention away from what we have to who we are. Then, that which is outside of us no longer threatens our interior.

The first effect of suffering is not purification but rather a kind of violence in which we keenly experience our attachment to the good that has been taken from us. Purification takes place in a kind of second step that forces us to exercise the powers of the soul. In interiority we measure, by resurrecting its presence within us, the value of the object we have lost. At this juncture spiritual activity may begin to function. We may realize our attachment to that which is outside of us and our lack of centering within. Perhaps, gradually we return to a solitude that is more than a mere empty exercise. Our solitude is not one that discards the human but rather distills the human. Through reflection we realize that that to which we are attached, namely intelligence or friends, are not our own by right but gifts to be reverenced, cared for and released. Solitude thus readies us to risk living again, even though such engagements with life may be painful.

It must be remembered that suffering of itself does not purify; no more than aloneness of itself is necessarily solitude. Every purification is realized by a reaction of the soul or the body, of which suffering is but the sign. Suffering can purify us only if it is accepted and only if there exists a real bond between it and the fault or weakness that is its source. This purification happens when suffering is engendered through the transforming power of reflection and when this suffering is willed, as well as, experienced. In other words, we are not indifferent to the suffering.

Rather, that which is born within us, because we willingly and humbly experience the pain and truth of suffering is that which heals us. Healing is an interior conversion of soul. Conversion cannot take place without the memory of the attachment or fault which caused the suffering, the mere representation of which is sufficient to make us suffer. Suffering is now one with purification. Unless we suffer for having committed an evil, we are not delivered from it.

Consequently, since suffering is an effect of reflection upon our involvement in evil, it can be the way to repentance. Even when remorse arises spontaneously, there is always in repentance, as in reflection, a kind of questioning of what has taken place and what we have done. It is not a remorseful imprisoning remembrance of the past but a repentance which looks to the past because we wish the future to be better. This experience has a liberating and purifying character because to have consciousness of the fault is already to have transcended it.

Reflections on Purification

An incident. "I only meant well. Why could she not see that? I'll show her. It will be a cold day in July when I next invite her family to have dinner with us. How can she be so unreasonable? "Such is my first reaction, a rather violent one, to the accusation of a friend who claims I coerced her family to stay and dine with us.

Only after I distance myself from the situation and from her do I begin to look at what part I had in the affair. I cease to concentrate exclusively on what I consider her injustice to me. Through reflection I begin to see that my main motivation for inviting her family was to repay the meals I had taken in her home. This was a chance to lessen my feeling of indebtedness to them. My insistence on their having dinner with us left them almost no alternative. The fact that this had not been a part of their plans and that today was an inopportune time since they were planning a birthday celebration, was not considered by me. Now, I begin to discern that I did indeed want my own way; that my way of getting it was selfish; and that my anger for the non-acceptance of my feigned good intentions manifested itself in hateful remarks. Gradually, I decide that I will act differently in the future. I realize that I must be less eager for what I want, merely because it satisfies me. I will be more caring for "the other" because I do love and respect her.

Centered in Self. A suffering, like the one described, can purify and change us but we have to take time for reflection; we must come home to ourselves. We cannot be continually caught up in that which is outside of us. We cannot judge our actions merely by how they are received. Rollo May says that to do so is to postpone judgment of the value of our actions until we look at the audience. If we act in this manner we tend to be mere performers in life rather than persons who live and act as selves.[2] Dag Hammarskjöld says something quite similar in these graphic lines from *Markings:*

> The little urchin makes a couple of feeble hops on one leg without falling down. And is filled with admiration at his dexterity, doubly so because there are onlookers. Do we ever grow up?[3]

To live healthily centered, we must foster an inner life through which we become aware of ourselves and our attachments or, as Lavelle says, turn our attention from what we have to who we are. We must experience our unique and real personhood. This means that we refuse to escape into a world of the "group" where we say and do the things that "they" applaud. We must be willing to "stand alone" and to accept responsibility for what we do. Having realized our selfish attachment, we affirm that which we value in opposition to it. This is an ongoing experience; repeated sufferings serve to remind us of our attachment.

Each time this attachment comes to our attention we are asked to choose again that which we profoundly value. In the foregoing incident, had I not been confronted, I may never have become conscious of my selfishness. By willingly taking the time and the energy for the reflection which was evoked by my hurt, the attachment to my desires is highlighted.

This distancing requires a certain vigilance and a willingness to ponder the undesirable reality of daily life. This vigilance ought to be lived in a relaxed way; that is, we do not expect ourselves or others to be perfect. As long as we are in this world, perfection is an impossibility. To expect perfection is to be doomed to failure. However, neither do we give up and simply expect others to accept us as we are.

Willing to be weak and yet willing to risk and hope for all, we embrace both the painful and joyful experiences of life. From the involvement of suffering we learn our attachments and hopefully allow suffering to purify us of them. By acknowledging the hold that past habits of behavior have upon us, we already begin to transcend them; we live more authentically both with ourselves and others. This proper psychological orientation fosters the creative life of the spirit.

It is further to be realized that this self, in its daily and full revelation, includes the sacred dimension. Gabriel Marcel states that our souls are made or unmade by the quality of our response to suffering.[4] In the next part we focus particularly on the suffering person and his relation to the sacred.

PART IV

SUFFERING IN RELATION TO THE SACRED

" . . . that there was in me . . . "

CHAPTER VIII

THE RELIGIOUS NATURE OF PERSON

The discussion of our religious nature is presented here in order to provide a basis for our remarks about suffering and its relation to us as religious persons.

At some time in our lives we experience the call of that which speaks of more than mere materiality. Perhaps we know it when we are surprised by the sunburst at dawn or look into the innocent, shining eyes of a baby. Or, like William Wordsworth, we may be moved to exclaim, "My heart leaps up when I behold a rainbow in the sky."[1]

Again, it may be that we recognize our spirit nature when we question. We may wonder about time and our inability to capture it or space and its immensity. With William Blake we may have questioned the source of the power, beauty and grandeur of life.

Tiger! Tiger! burning bright
In the forests of the night,
What immortal hand or eye
Dare frame thy fearful symmetry?[2]

Most of all we come in touch with that which is beyond and within ourselves when we experience selfhood in communion with others. No individual left to his own devices can cross the threshold that separates him from another. Nevertheless, there are times when a light breaks through and we discover another consciousness like ourselves. Even though we fear being unable to communicate with such a kindred spirit, our very fear may indicate that we are already close to meaningful presence.

In all of these experiences, the thrill of nature, questioning, human presence, there is an element of mystery. When we fail to see this mystery, we treat life as a problem. We do not reflect on life's deeper dimensions. Then we have only "business relations" and we use persons and things merely to serve our own ends.

A religious person respects life and its mystery. However, according to the Christian existentialist, Gabriel Marcel, contemporary man is no longer rooted in mystery.[3] Frequently, in present day culture the human person is regarded as but one object among the rest and is presented merely as a problem to be solved by technical methods alone. Marcel does not deny the value of the scientific and pragmatic intelligence, for there is a definite sense in which man is rightly included with the other things that are subject to technical control and measurement. However, this is not the only way in which man and other beings ought to be treated.

Man is both a thing and more than a thing, for he can undertake an evaluation of his own life. Such evaluation raises the question: who is it that asks about the meaning of his being and of the world? Who is it that calls this life into question? As we inquire about being we are ourselves an affirmation of being because only human beings can question.

The distinction between problem and mystery implies a distinction between scientific and philosophical knowledge.

A problem is that which can be inventoried, characterized and manipulated and is thus open to solution by the application of special techniques. Existential acts and the attitudes of persons cannot be handled as problems. These are of the nature of mystery.

Marcel defines a mystery as a problem that is constantly encroaching upon its own data and hence going beyond the condition of a problem. In the face of a problem, the investigator retains his superiority and distance. When this data is threatened by the direction of the study, then the threshold of mystery is crossed. Mystery designates the zone where the intellect acts in a new way in search of being. Mystery is constituted when we recognize man's participation in being as a creatively received gift from God.

It is through reflection that we know the divine source of the personal self. To enter into ourselves is to find the gift of being as it comes fresh from God's hands. It is to discover that we are not our own.

Mystery or the realm of being includes all things in the world so we do not need to escape from the senses in order to know being. Rather, to gain some understanding of being, we need a closer fidelity to these components of experience. The being studied in metaphysics is not a revealed mystery but a natural one. Through natural reflection on experience, in the Marcelian sense, we withdraw from the world in order to attach ourselves to the creative source of the world. We thus ally ourselves with the world from a divine perspective. We do not regard the world solely as an object of knowledge and control. As a participator in being, we are more intimately attached to the world than we would be if we took a purely problematic approach to it. Let us consider here how this might occur in our personal experience.

Experience of Being

> I am alone. The sun is hot but I have moved to the shade of a tree that hides the dirt road a half mile away and leaves only the tall grass, a lake and the trees beyond in my line of vision. Next to me a ladybug is scaling the tall blades of grass. The intricate pattern formed by the tips of a nearby weed attracts my attention. I look at it so long that it loses its identity and its silhouette seems detached from all else. The glistening water ripples slightly. Lazily lying back, I gaze only at the sky and the slowly moving clouds. Except for the buzz of industrious insects about me, the day is quiet. I came here when the sun was rising and now it is almost directly overhead.
>
> Within I am quiet, too. There is no planning, no deciding where I must be next, or what I want to get done. All seems as it ought to be, so in place. I, too, seem to blend and to be a part of nature. I feel at home.

Perhaps that is the freedom about which Marcel speaks. The freedom that allows me to choose the place that is already mine. Weeds, field flowers and the insects live in their place and each radiates a unique and special beauty.

I, free to choose to be what I am, frequently choose to be what I am not. Then, I experience myself as out of touch, as off center, as a foreigner to reality. Physically, I am sometime hyperactive and pushy and often tired. Mentally, I am anxious, demanding, controlling. I will to make my world. I do not respect the things about me for their own individual witness to being but rather handle them carelessly and unseeingly.

In the realm of things, consider, for example, a simple object like the pencil in my hand. What is it to me? Can it speak to me of more than materiality? A pencil, hard like my heart is so much of the time, hard like the firm support of a friend, useful because it serves as it is intended, useful but yet content to be laid aside for days, even years, waiting to be in the service of poetry or forgery, unable to resist because it lacks the freedom that is mine—a pencil is such a simple thing and yet I am so oblivious to the truth that it could teach me.

Consider again the wisdom that can be gained by contemplating the flower at my side. Alfred Tennyson reminds me of the truths it holds in these lines:

> Little flower,—but if I could understand
> What you are, root and all, and all in all,
> I should know what God and man is.[4]

Or, again from "Auguries of Innocence" by William Blake, the same truth is reiterated:

> To see the world in a grain of sand,
> And a heaven in a wild flower;
> Hold infinity in the palm of your hand,
> And eternity in an hour.[5]

Persons, even more than the things of nature, deserve my respect. Sometimes sharing with others has been a source of inspiration. At other times I have found such talk empty and dissipating. Perhaps this is true because I am not attentive to the other in a reverent way. Regardless of what another says, even should he speak of the weather, his word is in one sense inspirited. His truth and his way of expressing it is uniquely filled with life. Being inattentive, I may fail to treat him and his words with dignity.

Each of us is inspirited. We do not belong to ourselves alone. The originality which is ours is in one way greater than us. Our awareness of this truth may be a path to the divine source of our personal selves. For such revelation, we can only wait in an attitude of gratitude, openness, spontaneity and reverence. Such creative waiting will enable us to live our lives remembering and appreciating the mystery that is life. In thus respecting the mystery of all, we also respect the reality of suffering; we do not view suffering as a mere depreciation of self.

Rather, we allow suffering to gently beckon us home. We accept the reality of our finiteness and frailty which pain makes evident, thus surrendering to the infinite mystery that is us. We discover that there are infinite depths which we have only begun to sound and we realize that the immensity of all that is will never be known in its totality by us. By searching within, we come to experience Someone beyond. This Someone speaks to us through the everyday people, events and things in our lives, through our questioning. How is it that we are able to question? Why is it that we are constantly seeking? Why must we suffer? What within makes us search? Why is there anything at all? Why are we not like a stone, a tree, a dog? What is this mystery? What can we know about it? Perhaps that is a large part of the mystery—the fact that we cannot know in any sort of rational way. Even if we understand it, we cannot verbalize it. We can, however, live it. The mystery will permeate who we are and make us alive to all that is.[6]

CHAPTER IX

DISTORTED RELIGIOUS SUFFERING

Experiences of God are as diverse as the number of individuals who have in some way experienced God. For some, the "being" to which Marcel refers is identified with God; for others, "being" speaks of God's presence and yet for them God is more personal than "being". Our purpose here is not to discuss the various concepts and/or the numerous experiences of God but rather to look at suffering in relation to us as religious persons.

We saw that a problematic approach to life recognizes only a partial dimension of man's nature. Problems consider only questions such as "How fast does light travel?" or "How tall is the Washington monument?" or "In what century was the printing press invented?" Mystery, rather, is that which surrounds and permeates us. It concerns what we hold most intimate and most deep. If we attempt to treat suffering as a problem, our behavior in the face of it may be fatalistic, evasive, stoical or rebellious. To maintain a healthy balance in any area of life is a delicate endeavor. This is particularly true when we try to live pain and difficulty realistically.

Perhaps our childhood environment implied that suffering was good, or that suffering is a sign of God's love or disfavor. Or we may feel that if we are enjoying life, we are probably not very holy. Maybe in some subtle way we do believe as Mrs. Leivers philosophizes to Miriam in the movie, *Sons and Lovers,* "God made us to suffer." If so, we may tend to feel guilty whenever we are experiencing the exhilarating joy of being alive.

Unconsciously, we may even now use religious suffering as an "easy out" for avoiding the responsibility that life demands. For example, in the name of religion, we may inflict suffering on ourselves so as to alleviate guilt feelings or to escape honest confrontation with reality. We may even cling to suffering in order to feel holy or loved by God. Or, when suffering fills us with anguish at the death of a friend or dashes our dearest hopes to the ground, we may stoically deny the truth of what we feel and experience. We may even believe our pseudo resignation to God's Will is authentic religious behavior.

EXAMPLES OF SEEMINGLY PSEUDO "RELIGIOUS SUFFERING"

Distortion of religion is not only a common factor in our attitude toward suffering; it may also characterize the whole way we live the religious dimension of life. God may be merely a projection of our needs. Those "masters of suspicion," such as Freud, Nietzsche, Sartre, and Marx, do a service for us by focusing on the various false images of God through which we may deceive ourselves. They show us that God may be a mere projection of our father or Someone that we use to arouse guilt in others or a Refuge from freedom and responsibility.[1] Thus, true self emergence in relation to God can be furthered by reflecting on the distortions which may influence our lives. Our chief interest here is the way in which these misrepresentations of God may dominate our experience of suffering.

There are various historical examples of what seems to be a distorted religious approach to suffering. Reference to such historical perspectives can throw light on our heritage and thus indicate how the past still influences the present.

The experiences of religious suffering presented here are taken from mythology,[2] from American Indian practices and from more recent culture. Judgment of the motivations of the specific individuals who performed these rites is not intended. This material is discussed because, in a general way, it seems to emphasize a common mentality which makes religion synonymous with suffering. Following the presentation of these literary examples, the reflections clarify the subtle ways in which we, too, may identify religion and suffering.

Example from Mythology

The function of the gods in ancient Greek religion was to protect the complex state against political dangers. Belief in omens was universal and most calamities were attributed to offended or malevolent deities.[3] This is evidenced in Greek mythological literature, where responsibility for one's actions is abdicated by a constant blaming of the gods for the trouble.

This escape from responsibility is similar to the psychological defense mechanism of projection, the difference being that, instead of projecting the blame onto others, it is projected onto God. Man passively accepts and stoically endures the unpleasant reality of life as that which God wills. Consequently, he can refuse to responsibly improve unjust and painful situations in life and in the world. In fact, he may even consider himself more virtuous than those who do not live in such a resigned manner.

In the Iliad when the Trojans are defeating the Achaians, Aias, seeing that the victory is passing from them, remarks:

> Damn it, any fool can see that Father Zeus is

> helping the other side. All their shots hit, whether a good man throws or a bad man—Zeus makes 'em all go straight! And all ours miss and stick in the ground. . . .[4]

At another point in the story Achilles accepts the apology of Agamemnon and denounces his feud. Agamemnon, even in his final apology, defends his conduct by refuting those who say that it was all his fault in the following words:

> People have said that to me often enough, and reproached me, but it was not *my* fault—it was *their* fault! They put that blind madness in my heart amongst you all, on that day when I robbed Achilles of his prize myself. But what could I do? God bringeth all things to pass![5]

Such remarks are common throughout mythological writing and we will indicate later how they seem even to this day to represent a prevalent way of thinking.

Example from American Indian Culture

In the American Indian culture suffering and difficulties are often endured and even imposed so as to placate the spirits. Stoical endurance of some Indians is dramatized in the book *A Man Called Horse.*

Here, Joe Walking Wolf, upon hearing that a friend has been wounded in war, asks Charley Lockjaw to teach him the hard ceremony of swinging at the pole. Joe Walking Wolf expresses his motivation in these words:

> . . . Tom Little Hand has a bad wound, and he

> is my friend. I will make this sacrifice because it will help him get well. Anyway, I will know what it is to be wounded. I did not go to war.[6]

The ceremony consists of swinging from a lariat that has been fastened to a pole in the ground. The skin on Joe's shoulders is pinched and with a sharp knife a tunnel is made for three-inch skewers. Over each skewer is placed a loop of rawhide which is tied to the lariat that hangs from the pole. Joe walks a quarter of a circle to the right four times and back, sagging forward hard on the lariat, trying to tear the skewers through. Then, he walks to the left. This procedure continues all day stopping only three times before the sun goes down to smoke a pipe. Joe walks and pulls mightily but he cannot break through the tough flesh that stretches like rubber. The flesh is not broken when the sun sets but Charley now cuts him free and Joe is still with honor. Joe does not even heave a sigh to show his relief that this suffering is over.

Another example of imposed pain occurs when Pretty Calf mourns her brother's death. She is described as cutting off chunks of her long hair and crying as she gashes her arms with a knife. In the time of mourning the family of the deceased makes itself poor. Every thing that means comfort, wealth and safety is sacrificed to the spirits. In addition to these sacrifices, Pretty Calf's mother, Greasy Hand, cuts off a joint of her finger at the death of each son. Finally at the death of her daughter, Pretty Calf, she cannot remove a finger joint or she will no longer be able to work.

Such ceremonial suffering is not foreign even today. We may obviously or subtly impose suffering on ourselves, thus hoping to ease guilt feelings for past and/or present neglect. Before illustrating this let us recount a literary example which is situated in the more recent past.

Example from Middle-Class Culture

In the autobiographical book *Of Human Bondage,* W. Somerset Maugham tells the story of a club-footed boy, Philip, whose deformity is a source of horrible sensitivity. After his mother's death, young Philip goes to live with his uncle, the Vicar, who is a proud, egotistical, holier-than-thou minister of the church.

The author relates several incidents which show that the Vicar seems to identify religion with somberness and suffering. On one Sunday afternoon Philip is playing with toy bricks which suddenly fall in noisy ruin and awaken his uncle. The Vicar is irritated and harshly scolds Philip:

> Don't you know it's very, very, wicked to play on Sunday? What d'you suppose it's called the day of rest for? You're going to church tonight, and how can you face your Maker when you've been breaking one of His laws in the afternoon?[7]

Later in the story, Philip prays fervently to be cured and fixes a date for the miracle. His little room is icy and he shivers when he puts on his nightshirt. But, Maugham tells us, " . . . he always felt that his prayers were more pleasing to God when he said them under conditions of discomfort. The coldness of his hands were an offering to the Almighty."[8]

Even though little Philip prays to be made sound this novel seems to reiterate the belief, which has been instilled into young Philip by the Vicar, that God is indeed happy if he is miserable.

REFLECTIONS ON PSEUDO RELIGIOUS SUFFERING

In our reflections on the foregoing examples, three distortions of religious suffering are evident: a fatalistic escape into "God's Will"; an evasive isolation which may be falsely considered a prelude to mystical experience; and a stoical martyr complex which sometimes is the basis of a rebellious holier-than-thou attitude.

Fatalistic Escape into "God's Will"

It is true that for the man of faith God's loving Providence is manifested in every moment of life. However, a resigned attitude which proclaims that every suffering is God's Will and that, therefore, there is nothing we can do to change a situation may be fatalistic. Unconsciously, such an attitude may be a justification for doing our own will or it may be a passive stance that assures us of having to do nothing. Like the characters in Homer's *Iliad,* we may be trying to escape responsibility for the insufficiency that our suffering presents. Because the Trojans are victorious over the Greeks, the Greeks, rather than accept the superiority of the opposing army, choose to place the responsibility for their defeat on God.

Similarly, we may not have the courage or the conviction needed to confront unjust situations or structures within our family, business, church or government. However, rather than admit that we fear conflict or rejection we may abdicate responsibility and baptize this behavior by crediting our societal injustices to God. In this way we absolve ourselves from effort and simultaneously salve our conscience with the bromide, "It is God's Will!"[9] A more involved and life giving response might be to make honest though perhaps painful, strained and, at times, even mistaken efforts to build a just society.

Or, we may cast off responsibility in the name of religion by excusing ourselves from the study, hard work or practice necessary to achieve our goals when the real truth may be we prefer a lackadaisical, self-centered, undisciplined life. At other times, we may justify our overwork by pseudo religious motivations. There are so many people who want to talk to us about their problems or need us in another fashion. God makes continual demands upon us, so we think. Failing to look beyond the surface, we may never realize that we are placing these demands on ourselves.

Evasive Isolation

We may use other subtle ways to avoid difficult situations. For example, we may rationalize our unwillingness to participate in school or civic community endeavors by expounding that we can only relate with those who believe as we do. Since this group has not yet elicited our trust, we isolate ourselves from them. The truth may be that we are unwilling to have our ideas contradicted or to work through the conflict that honest involvement with others often demands.

Because we also have a need for togetherness, we may vacillate between a closed distant stance and an open friendly manner. We thus leave others bewildered as to our true intentions by beckoning them with one hand and shoving them away with the other. Our inconsistency and our refusal to become personally involved may eventually cut off the very persons who could lessen our isolation.

Then living isolated from others becomes a way of life for us. We may even label our selfish isolation "solitude" and equate this "solitude" with the distancing required for mystical experiences. Perhaps in our isolation, we live in a religiously sacrificial manner hoping to reduce the guilt which haunts us for being selfishly and fearfully uninvolved.

Possibly Joe Walking Wolf experienced a similar form of guilt in being isolated from his wounded friend who fought in the war. By suffering or punishing himself he may have felt the relief that we experienced as children when we were spanked for wrong doing. In various ways, we, may even now be punishing ourselves for a guilt and shame that we refuse to name or admit to ourselves. However, if we can honestly face our motivations and own our sins, we may realize both our need for God's forgiveness, as well as, our need to forgive ourselves. Then our aloneness gradually becomes a solitude that prepares us for meaningful involvement where suffering is more redemptive than punitive.

Stoical Martyr-Complex

True stoics accept and endure. For a person without Christian faith, stoicism seems to be the most fitting attitude toward suffering. It would seem that stoicism colored the behavior of the Indians described earlier. Yet, Thomas Merton tells us that "To accept suffering stoically, to receive the burden of the unavoidable and to bear it strongly, is no consecration."[10] Stoicism, at times, seems to be identified with an attitude stiffened by pride and defiance.

As long as we can congratulate ourselves for bearing up strongly under suffering, we really have not yet experienced the full impact of suffering. We are still masters of the situation. It is when we experience weakness and inability to suffer well that we realize who we are, namely, limited creatures. Humbly, we may then turn to others for support and yet ultimately find that we are alone in this very painful experience that has impinged upon our lives.

Self pity also stems from a martyr complex. When this self pity is verbalized, the recital of our woes may terminate with the prosaism, "I suffer all of this cheerfully because I want only to do God's Will." At another time when criticized or confronted by others we feign docility to show how Christlike we are. Later, our moodiness and repressed hostility spreads gloom all about us. Prolonged brooding frequently magnifies the initial incident and thus we feed our martyr-complex. Perhaps it is this self-pity thriving on others' sympathy, that initiates a certain rebellious holier-than-thou behavior.

Holier-than-thou Attitude

"What are you doing here?" is the bitter reaction to another's friendly, "Good Morning." We just cannot stand her nonchalant manner, her smoking and drinking, her sexy walk and most of all her lack of religious penance and devotion. Fortunately, we know her kind so she doesn't have a chance with us. Strangely though, she never seems to catch on that we do not want her around. She continues to ask about our work and health. We answer her, if at all, in monosyllables and then we make subtle references about the terrible sinfulness in the world and about our dedicated love for the Church. We hope our remarks help her realize that not everyone lives as she does. Our attitude here is similar to the proud stoical behavior of the Vicar in Maugham's novel.

Hopefully, we eventually question our own behavior. We may wonder if our coldness and dislike of others is due to the fact that we want what they enjoy. Perhaps we are envious because we are dissatisfied with our own lives. We may rightly be wary of our escape into supposedly religious behavior through which we hide bitter resentment even from ourselves. Or, we may suspect our former rationalizations which claimed we were better if we spent hours in Church work while another did little if anything for the Church; if we attended daily services while others did well to go on Sunday, and if we used our time visiting the sick while they played tennis. We may begin to realize that we could be denying ourselves rigorously for the wrong reasons and discover that we are pleasing ourselves mightily with our self-denial.

CONCLUSION

Using religion as a "cop-out" in avoiding the risks and pain of life is a common escape for those who are supposedly living a religious life. Phony religiosity may insidiously and elusively color attitudes and stymie personal growth. The more positive we are that such false motivation is not ours, the more likely is it to be so. It is precisely this outward show of religion that makes the detection of double-mindedness difficult.

However, all is not lost. By willingly and honestly exploring our motivation we can live a more authentic and happy life. We ought not judge others' motives but periodically we must be willing to examine our own. Perhaps in reality we have identified religion with pain and made God merely a caricature of the stern father. Often the remarks of those who live closest to us can be a means of learning the truth about ourselves. Considering, too, why we are bothered by another or upset by a particular situation may be revealing. In the next chapter we discuss this positive religious way of assuming suffering.[11]

CHAPTER X

POSITIVE VALUE OF SUFFERING FOR THE RELIGIOUS PERSON

> Suffering does not diminish us but reveals us to ourselves . . . . There are thresholds that thought, left to its own resources, can never cross; an experience is needed, poverty, sickness . . . . It is as if our eyes are opened and we can see things that we never even dreamed. Perhaps the world itself is given another dimension.[1]

The philosopher, Jean Vieujean, reiterates the above truth when he says, "There is much in us, but it often takes some obstacle, accident, opposition, or hardship to reveal it to us."[2]

Concretely, the truth of these statements is revealed in the life of the invalid, France Pastorelli. She was a gifted musician whose state of health put a stop to all musical activity. At each dawn she struggled to give up what she loved and could no longer have. Continually regretting that her highest ideal seemed unrealizable, she nevertheless desired not to fall short of what her destiny demanded and not to lose what God had revealed to her in suffering.[3]

She recalls days that stand out as brilliantly as a beacon of fire, days of absolute immobility and extreme weakness, when reading, writing and talking were impossible, when the noise of people coming and going, however careful they were, was intolerable. Her power of thought at this time, far from being exhausted like her body, was intensified as she states, "beyond belief." The impossibility of leading an active life set free an extraordinarily enhanced capacity for thought and feeling with which nothing could interfere. In such hours France lived a strange and exalted life, in which she felt that she had reached the zenith of her moral sensibility, the spiritual peak where all the powers of thought and the capacity for love was increased tenfold. She says, too, that if the soul does indeed exist, then she has "touched" it at such moments. In any case, she holds that she was conscious of it in a way that she had never been when leading a normal existence and that she felt her soul grew in her like a body in gestation.[4] Indeed, suffering brought her, as Marcel states in the initial quote, to thresholds that thought left to itself could not cross.

Ordinarily suffering is not so intensely and exquisitely experienced by most persons. Often, in fact, we are angered by it. Like the wounded veteran interviewed by Gordon Allport, we may despair and reject God when confronted with suffering. This devout veteran was praying while waiting to attack the enemy. At that very moment a bomb burst close by. He lost one arm, was disfigured and blinded. The wounded man became a total and militant atheist. Allport tells of yet another blinded veteran who reported that his handicap brought him inner light and peace, as well as, an awakened faith.[5]

What fosters the attitudes that enhance the person rather than embitter? Experientially, positive attitudes seem to be nurtured by a free exploration of negative thought and feelings. The negative quandry proposed by C.S. Lewis may at times be experienced by all of us:

> If God were good, He would wish to make His creatures perfectly happy, and if God were almighty He would be able to do what He wished.

> But the creatures are not happy. Therefore God lacks either goodness, or power, or both.[6]

Since such a dilemma troubles many people, let us consider it here in the light of observations made by Vieujean.

REFLECTION ON GOD'S POWER AND GOODNESS

Vieujean[7] asks that we first consider what is meant by the words, "all-powerful," "good," "happy." When we want to grasp adequately what words and ideas express, we must purify and spiritualize our whole being. Even then, words remain cut to the measure of human things. They are powerless to express God as He is, hence, when we apply them to Him, we must always do it with prudence and humility. In God everything takes on a "more" and "different" infinity.

The power of God. When we say that God is all powerful, we mean his power surpasses the power of creatures completely. His power is of another order and cannot be measured with the power of creatures. It outclasses the power of creatures in three ways: 1) God alone can create, that is, make whatever is not, be and exist; 2) God can interfere with secondary causes, namely, his creatures through miraculous power; and 3) God can make us participate in his intimate life and lift us above created possibilities by his supernatural power.

What God Cannot Do. The power of God does not give him the capacity to make a square circle nor a cubic sphere; or a road which would go uphill but which would not come down. From the moment that God created secondary causes, that is, beings engaged in particular activities, it was natural that He would let them act on their own dynamism and not intervene at times to suspend their activity and change their ways.

Yes, God made us free. We are capable of using the world with prudence, charity and detachment. We have the choice, not the right, to use the world with indulgence, imprudence, selfishness, drunkenness and even idolatry.

We may insist that if God were all-powerful, he would be able to correct the results each time we abuse our free will,

> so that a wooden beam became soft as grass when it was used as a weapon, and the air refused to obey me if I attempted to set up in it the sound waves that carry lies or insults. But such a world would be one in which, wrong actions were impossible, and in which, therefore, freedom of will would be void; nay, if the principle were carried out to its logical conclusion, evil thoughts would be impossible; for the cerebral matter which we use in thinking would refuse its task when we attempted to frame them.[8]

Miracles and Their Purpose. Being all-powerful, God can perform miracles. He can suspend or change the causalities common to creatures. God could not prevent all evil without transforming the world into a theatre of puppets where secondary causes would be unable to exercise their own energy. Even when miracles do occur, it *does not* seem that God is pursuing the suppression of suffering through these miracles as His primary end. Rather, it would seem that He wants to manifest His paternal presence to men and by a sign, He attracts their attention. Miracles are rare and are kept relatively quiet and hidden. They are an awakening, an invitation to watchfulness and not a sledge-hammer blow which would knock out the spirit and force it to surrender.

Vieujean concludes his discussion of miracles by stating that the more we love the divine will, even when it is difficult, the less we need miraculous signs and the more God becomes light, near present. On the contrary, the less we seek to transform our hearts and live by the Spirit of God, the more we need miracles.

With this background regarding the nature of God's power, a nature that respects the freedom of our persons, we now consider the mystery of suffering.

REFLECTIONS ON THE MYSTERY OF SUFFERING

No words sufficiently explain suffering. In the experience of suffering, the presence of others may be supportive. Nonetheless, intrinsically we suffer alone. Continually, unanswerable questions and indescribable agony of mind or body remind us that suffering has no explanation and seems indeed to be a mystery.

This mystery baffles us and in another sense can fill us, as does the mystery of life, with a certain awe and respect. If we regard life's mystery, all the things we have or receive; all the people who enter, mark, and perhaps leave our lives; all the events both happy and sad, that are a part of our experience are reverenced as the gifts they are. We live our lives in gratitude for all the daily, hourly and even momentary love that we experience. Thus we do not focus on what is absent, that which our desires tell us we must have, but on what is present, the many blessings of the now.

We have been gifted by being given life. So many other possible beings have not been actualized. We are creatures; we are limited. We are not meant to cling to, to calculatively control, nor to manage this mysterious gift of life. Thus to live fully, we must have an open hand, taking in but also releasing and letting go. Some call this the rhythm of involvement and detachment.

Concretely, how might we experience this dynamic interplay in suffering? Living life's mystery means that we involve ourselves with others and at the same time be willing to live the risk and hurt of loving them. This does not mean that we brace ourselves in anticipation of their departure nor do we submit to inevitable hurt fatalistically.

Rather, when separated from another in whatever way, even by death, we can be grateful for what has been while living the pain of what is. Strictly speaking, we had no right to share another person's life. His friendship was and is gift. For this mutuality we can be thankful. We can rejoice in the times we roamed the hills, admired the shimmer on the lake, prayed together in the quiet of the evening, and silently touched and knew the oneness of our persons. Such memories remind us that we will always be a part of each other. Even now we do not know what marvels the mystery of life still holds. Living in a receptive way, we are willing to take in and freely let go again all which gratuitously enhances our lives.

This receptivity does not happen easily and we do not wish *to minimize* the difficulty of saying "yes" everyday of our lives for years on end. The temptation to give in to bitterness and discouragement, as well as the tragic shattering loneliness that grips one in the face of suffering are too real to be passed over lightly. It would be simplistic to believe that any words could explain or remove suffering. As has been said earlier, suffering is indeed a mystery and as long as we live authentically it will continue to thwart and confront us.

In the dramatic poem, *Samson Agonistes,* John Milton conveys some of the intensity and struggle that accompanies living this mystery of suffering. We consider it here because it exemplifies how suffering can be the path to rebirth and redemption.

REFLECTIONS ON MILTON'S SAMSON AGONISTES[9]

Briefly, *Samson Agonistes* is the story of biblical Samson who because he is unfaithful to God loses his strength. After his capture by the Philistines, he grievously suffers and finally repents of his disloyalty to God. His strength is restored and when he is brought to the feast, proclaimed by the Philistines as a day of thanksgiving for their deliverance from Samson's hands, he destroys the place of feasting and also himself. Thus he gives his life to rid his people of their enemies, the Philistines.

This account is seriously and intensely related by the sensitive visionary, Milton, who himself suffered much. Though naturally inclined to be a poet, he temporarily put aside this inclination in order to further the rights of the common man. However, when the English monarchy was restored, Milton saw much of his life's work in the interest of the common man destroyed. This experience, as well as his blindness in later life, evidences Milton's personal suffering.

Samson Is a Prototype of All Men

The compactness of the poem heightens the union of past, present and future and intimates that every decision we make in life has meaning in terms of our life as a whole. And, since there is little mention of Samson's specific physical features or his individual personal characteristics, it is easier to identify with Samson as a representative of every man.

Through the poem we experience Samson's purgation and illumination, his fall and his redemption. His is a noble redemption which is the fruit of temptations overcome and suffering embraced. The term "agonistes" itself, in its older form meant a physical combat and later it came to mean a spiritual struggle. Milton's emphasis is on the spiritual struggle of a tragic hero, Samson.

Samson's Experience of Suffering

The poem begins with a description of a dismal blind Samson, imprisoned and afflicted with multiple and forever-present thoughts of the dereliction that has befallen him. His mental anguish is caused to a great extent by the scoffing of others and his own inability to see meaning in his suffering. As an onlooker, we, like those in the chorus, can more easily see meaning in his suffering and we hope that he will courageously face each crisis. Samson, however, does not have the same vantage point.

Gradually he does realize that his present situation in prison is really not so base as his former self-indulgent life. He recalls his proud display of herculean strength in the face of his present weakness and confronted with his insufficiency, he accepts his creatureliness. He admits that he is guilty before God and man and that he has been disloyal to both.

In admitting his guilt Samson is rewarded with moral insight. Samson knows that the cause of his suffering is not God but rather his own unfaithfulness to that which is most truly himself. In selfishly refusing to listen to and follow the deeper call of his life, he has distorted and disregarded the reality within that summons him. Though Samson himself cannot advance toward God, divine justice can advance toward him.

Through his repentance Samson is brought to a kind of calm and resignation. This resignation does not mean that he no longer suffers. Rather, in discerning through his suffering the truth about himself, he seeks God's friendship in his misery. He now has hope and sees purpose in his suffering and hence actually suffers less. He proves his willingness to be faithful to God by embracing his suffering and allowing it to purify him.

He does not seek to escape it, although opportunities to do so are presented to him. For example, Samson is urged to choose an easier alternative by Manoa, his father, who has made arrangements with some Philistian lords to ransom him. Dalila, too, insistently proposes to Samson a way to escape his suffering. Craftily, she offers to serve him with redoubled love and care until his old age if he will leave with her. Momentarily it seems to Dalila that Samson doubts his own wisdom and she further pressures Samson through sensuous charm to forsake his faith and escape his present suffering, "let me approach at least, and touch thy hand".

However, Samson, aware of Dalila's trickery, is not deceived. Since his repentance he is ruled by higher aspirations and he repudiates her seductive behavior:

> Not for thy life, lest fierce remembrance wake
> My sudden rage to tear thee joint by joint,
> at distance I forgive thee, go with that;

In similar instances, we unlike Samson, may listen to

such rationalization and accept that which others and our culture urge, so as to escape suffering. In so doing, we may be unfaithful to our true self. That which challenges us and, at times, necessarily demands suffering, we may rationalize as inhuman. Insisting that we must be ourselves, we may mean that we must act the way we feel. True, feelings, being neither good nor bad, tell us much about ourselves so we must name our feelings and accept them as our own. However, being free, we can decide how we will respond to them. Many times each day, we, as responsible persons, choose a more burdensome and painful path contrary to the path that our feelings may dictate. Like repentant Samson, we opt to be faithful to ourselves and to trust a Power beyond us.

Gradually our suffering may purify and strengthen us, for by willingly losing ourselves we gain our true selves. Ours, too, may be a new vision. Samson was born again through the reflective inwardness initiated by suffering. His deeper penetration of life led him to wisdom and greater spiritual maturity. Through his utter aloneness, through his having been thrown back on his own resources, he slowly turned to God and was then able to surrender expectantly to his destiny. For Samson, "weakness," evidenced in his suffering proved to be true spiritual strength, by which he was able to accomplish his original task and to save his people. Paradoxically, it served him better than intelligence or even virtue.

In a kind of identification with Samson in his weakness we know our need for redemption. Thus we are encouraged by the Chorus in these final reflections:

> All is best, though we oft doubt,
> What the unsearchable dispose

Of highest wisdom brings about,
And ever best found in the close.
Oft he seems to hide his face,
But unexpectedly returns
And to his faithful Champion hath in place
Bore witness gloriously; . . . .

CONCLUSION

Of its very nature, mystery is elusive and incomprehensible. The wonder aroused by a glowing sunset or a majestic mountain is one such experience of mystery. Full awareness, however, includes the mysterious capacity for misery, as well as for happiness. The optimist sees pain as the complement of love and is inclined to call these the wings on which our spirit can best take flight toward the Absolute. Pain plunges like a sword through creation leaving on one side cringing and degraded animals and on the other heroes and saints. And, just as we cannot understand why great poetry moves us to unspeakable emotions, neither can we know why in religion, in pain and in beauty, persons insist that they recognize at least a glimpse of the Real.

As Christians, we are graced to live this mystery of suffering through the added support of faith, a faith which is deepened as we live more intimately with Christ and is of the essence of Christian life. It is this faith-life in relation to suffering that we ponder in the next Chapter.

PART V

CHRISTIAN SUFFERING

". . . an Invincible Summer."

CHAPTER XI

A CHRISTIAN INCARNATES GOD IN THIS WORLD

> Now we are seeing a dim reflection in a mirror;
> then we shall be seeing face to face. (1 Cor. 13:12)

> This, in fact, is what you were called to do
> because Christ suffered for you and left an
> example for you to follow the way he took.
> (1 Peter 2:21)

To trust the dim reflection, to believe that then we shall see face to face, is the blessing of faith, for without faith, suffering is little more than a curse. As Merton remarks, with faith, we can see our trials

> not as the collision of my life with a blind machine called fate, but as the sacramental gift of Christ's love, given to me by God the Father along with my identity and my very name, then I can consecrate them and myself with them to God. For then I realize that my suffering is not my own. It is the Passion of Christ stretching out its tendrils into my life in order to bear rich clusters of grapes, making my soul dizzy with the wine of Christ's love, and

> pouring that wine as strong as fire upon the whole world.[1]

In this succinct summary on suffering, Merton insists that Christianity has the potential to transform and enhance our living of the mystery of suffering. This mystery, the focus of reflection in the previous two chapters is experienced in varying degrees by most of us. At least we are capable of experiencing mystery. However, to live the suffering mystery in a Christian way, we must be gifted with faith. Faith strengthens us to believe in a personal God who is revealed through the Father as Creator, through Christ as Redeemer and through the Holy Spirit as Inspirer. In Sacred Scripture these and other Christian beliefs are further developed and explained.

The revealed truths which pertain to the baptized Christian as he experiences suffering are the main considerations in this section. Specifically, the truths discussed are these:

1. The mystery of human suffering only makes ultimate sense when seen with the eyes of faith.
2. Though sin brought suffering into the world, through this "happy fault" Christ's love also came into our lives.
3. Through finding ourselves in Christ and uniting our suffering with His we can come to know and share with others a personal God who is made visible in the everydayness of life.

These three realities parallel the three aspects of suffering which have been central throughout this book, namely: faith-inwardness; sinfulness-limitation; union with

Christ-attitude. Here we refer to them briefly and hope that as this chapter develops the correlation will be clarified. Though faith is a gift, it roots and anchors itself in our natural interiority or inwardness; sinfulness makes us concretely aware of our limitations; and union with Christ's Passion definitely influences our attitude toward suffering. Hence, the three aspects emerge—The inwardness we experience in suffering discloses our limitations and in this inner reflective stance we determine our attitude.

BELIEVING INVOLVES LOSING AND FINDING OURSELVES IN CHRIST

Selected Reflections on Suffering as Presented by Thomas Merton

Faith. Thomas Merton[2] states nothing so easily becomes unholy as suffering, and that if we are Christians, we must not only accept suffering, but must also make it holy. It is through faith that suffering is consecrated to God. This is a faith not in suffering but in God.

Suffering has no power or value of its own. To believe merely in suffering as suffering, is pride; but to suffer believing in God, is humility. Faith knows that the mercy of God is given in suffering and that His grace can overcome evil with good. Suffering, then, becomes good by accident because suffering can make us able to receive more abundantly from the mercy of God. What we consecrate to God in suffering is not our suffering but ourselves.

Sin and the love of Christ. A society whose whole idea is to eliminate suffering and bring its members the greatest amount of comfort and pleasure is doomed to be destroyed, so says Merton. Not all suffering is necessarily to be avoided. Nor is suffering the only evil, as our world often thinks. Sometimes it is absolutely necessary to face suffering, which is a lesser evil, in order to avoid or to overcome the greatest evil, sin.

We are created to will what God wills; to know what He knows and to love what He loves. Sin is the will to do what God does not will, to know what He does not know and to love what He does not love. Therefore, every sin is a sin against obedience, truth and love. Sin thus proves itself to be a supreme injustice not only against God, but above all, against ourselves.

We are saved from sin by the sufferings of Christ. His death on the cross has an infinite meaning and value not because it is a death, but because it is the redemptive death of the Son of God. It is also a sign which speaks of the power of Him who overcame both suffering and death by rising from the grave.

The saint responds to this love of Christ by being so attuned to the spirit and heart of Christ that he is compelled to answer the demands of love by a love that matches that of Christ. For the saint love is deep, so personal and so exacting that it becomes his whole destiny. The more he answers the secret action of Christ's love in his heart, the more he comes to know love's inexorable demands and the more he discovers his true creative self.

Find ourselves in Christ. When suffering puts the question, "Who are You?" to us, we must be able to answer and give our name. By this Merton means that we must express the very depths of what we are, what we have desired to be, what we have become. All of these things are sifted out by pain, and they are often found to be in contradiction with one another. However, if we live as Christians, our name and work and personality will fit the pattern of Christ stamped on our souls at Baptism.

In the sacramental character of Baptism we receive a name which gives us our identity and the divine vocation to find ourselves in Christ. Our Baptism, so to speak, drowns us in the death of Christ and summons upon us all the sufferings of life. These sufferings help us work out the pattern of our identity. If, therefore, we desire to be what we are meant to be and if we become what we are supposed to become, the questioning of suffering will call forth from us both our name and the name of Jesus. Through our suffering experience, we begin to work out our destiny which is to become one with Christ. We realize that we live now, not with our own life but with the life of Christ who lives in us. (Gal. 2:20)

Personal Reflections on Christian Suffering

Faith in Christ. Without faith, human suffering is only an intolerable burden. On the contrary, it is through suffering that faith is often strengthened. To speak of faith in its deepest meaning is to imply "faith in someone." Who is this someone that we, as Christians, believe in?

Too quickly and too glibly, we perhaps respond, "Christ." But do we know Him of whom we speak? Have there not been moments when we have had to admit, at least to ourselves, that we do not know Christ? Yet, is that really so strange? Are we not always coming to know the mystery of person, the person of Christ? In one way we do know Christ. We do not know Him in any sort of total and final way. We cannot write a concise paragraph and thus finally answer the question, "Who Is Christ?" Such would be a problematic approach to the mystery of Christ.

No, knowing Christ is a love story to which we never write

the final word or perhaps we write only a few words. Though we cannot definitively say who Christ is, we know something about Him. We can reflect on our momentary glimpses of Him which are similar to our insights into the persons we love. When we attempt to verbalize these, we may be disappointed. "No, that is not what I want to say, that is not how it is," we find ourselves saying. The words do not really convey the full truth of experience.

And, this is where faith enters the picture. If we fully knew Him, we would have no need for faith. We would not flee Him, "down the nights and down the days; down the arches of the years; or down the labyrinthine ways of my own mind."[3] as Francis Thompson so poignantly expresses in "The Hound of Heaven." Rather than flee, the strength of faith moves us beyond fear and indifference to seeking Him instead. Could it be that, at times, we look for him where he cannot be found? Are we seeking merely a fantasied historical Christ? Will we ever find the manly Christ that walked the Palestinian roads? In one sense, yes, that is if we let Him reveal Himself as He wishes to be known through His word. Somehow He touches us there. We touch Him and wonder why "Who is Christ?" is even a question.

We also know Christ as incarnate. He is God-with-us. Questioning in what sense this is true, we are faced again with mystery. At times we know His presence through our senses, or our rationality or through an all-pervasive experience of being. Hence, we find Him all about us, speaking through the things, persons and events of our lives. We do not discover Him only in that which is outside of us but, as has been said, we may know Him in the very depths and aloneness of our separate selves.

Obsession with finding a final answer to the Christ question may be a form of pride, a refusal to live by faith.

Knowing Christ, includes a willingness to live mystery and to breathe deeply in faith. With Kierkegaard, our frequent prayer might be, "Teach me, O God, not to torture myself, not to make a martyr out of myself through stifling reflection, but rather teach me to breathe deeply in faith."[4] Faith is both tested and called forth in the suffering experience—a reality we will explore more fully in the next chapter.

Sin and Christ's love. It is faith then that Christ demands. Listen to Him as He addresses the unbelieving Jews, " . . . Yes, if you do not believe that I am He, you will die in your sins." (John 8:24) Suffering is a consequence of sin. This is not to say that suffering is a punishment for sin but rather that it is the result of wrong doing. Unbelievers know the evil of sin but are without hope. Believing is to trust in Christ. It is to know the evil of sin and yet to recognize the greater glory of the redemption by which we are saved from sin.

We know the fruits of the redeeming Passion by His great love which is manifested in all of life. Ladislaus Boros says that knowing in biblical language means "two beings becoming one in love."[5] Thus, Boros, like Merton, says, everything that Christ bears within Himself becomes ours. This is to say, the whole cosmos, all the richness and beauty of the earth, and the Holy Trinity becomes ours in loving union.

Already now we bear all that richness within us but not yet openly. In Heaven it will be part of our nature, lived, felt, experienced and real. As John says in his first epistle,

> My dear people, we are already the children of God but what we are to be in the future has not yet been revealed; all we know is that when it is revealed we

> shall be like Him, because we shall see Him as He really is. (I John 3:2)

Finding ourselves in the everyday losing of self.

We participate in the personal reality of Christ by reenacting the whole redeeming act of Christ, i.e. by the death-rebirth cycle of the Christian. Nonetheless, the Passion and Resurrection, when considered in relation to Christ's whole life, was not the whole of His earthly life.

Most of Christ's life, like ours, was a hidden life. We, too, participate in His personal everyday reality by lovingly and wholesomely living everydayness as He did His at Nazareth.

The genuine discovery of Christ in daily life is not a flight from self. We cannot discover God in ourselves and ourselves in Him unless we have the courage to face ourselves exactly as we are, with all our limitations, and to accept others as they are, with all their limitations.

One evidence of our acceptance of others is our selfless grateful concern for them. Keeping our life only for ourselves tends to harden and deaden life. Essentially, we become ourselves by giving up ourselves. For example, by forgetting and giving up our pride, we may put aside the sullen silence of hurt feelings. The giving up of self is a giving up, then, of selfish ego clutching.

Giving up the ego self which is the source of true compassion is not easily lived.[6] So quickly it can become condescension or saccharine niceness. One example of genuine compassion is described in the novel, *The Woman Who Was Poor.* Gacougnol, the painter, expresses real concern for Clotilde, a poor deserted creature, whose body in one sense is not even her own. Evil Chapius, posing as

Clotilde's father, makes a monetary arrangement with Gacougnol to have Clotilde model in the nude.

Though this work is extremely distasteful to reserved Clotilde, she can see no alternative but to obey Chapius since he lives with and supposedly supports her widowed mother and herself.

When Clotilde arrives for the sitting, Gacougnol, unaware of Clotilde's delicate sensitivity, asks her to disrobe and continues his conversation with a caller. Later he notices that she is only partially undressed and is crying. He inquires, "My child—why are you crying?"[7] Quickly recognizing why, he begins to blame himself for his lack of sensitivity and kindly tells her that he intended no offense. Though to some, Gacougnol's words may sound brusque, his seeming nonchalant rambling is filled with gentle compassion for Clotilde. His understanding and respect for her who ordinarily experiences only hate and abuse is apparent in the following rapid flow of words:

> Cover up your shoulders, . . . and come and sit down here by the fire. Let's just have a quiet chat, like old friends. Don't try to speak yet, but do please just try and wipe your eyes dry. I may be a bit of a brute, but I can't quite bear to see you crying. I just can't help it. Look here! You're scared of posing for me 'altogether', isn't that it? I understand. If I had taken a better look at you when you came, I should have spoken to you differently. You mustn't be hurt with me. It's one's work makes one like that. If you only knew the drabs that come along to pose or do whatever else one likes! They don't cry, give you my word, at taking off their chemises!—and it isn't always very

lovely or very stimulating when they've got 'em off! Besides, one was a bit put out over something else. You saw me talking to that conceited idiot just now? Well, there you are! One gets into the way of riding the high horse, mixing with those asses—and sometimes one puts one's foot in it. Anyhow, you're not cross, are you?[8]

Bloy says that Clotilde was "vividly aware of the compassion of this good man, blaming himself for the sake of reassuring her!"[9] Gacougnol further tries to excuse his rude manner by telling Clotilde of his agreement with Chapius and how it had not prepared him to meet someone such as she.

. . . The beggar talked about you as if you were goods for sale . . . You can see, little girl, the way this inauspicious preliminary did not quite prepare me beforehand to hand out exaggerated salutations to you.[10]

Continuing, Gacougnol proposes an alternate plan which he presents to Clotilde without being ingratiating,

But don't let's talk about it. Here is my idea. Will you pose for the head only? You've got a saint's face that I've been looking for for months. I'll give you three francs an hour. That suit you? Mind, I'm asking it as a favour—[11]

There can be no question that this is satisfactory to Clotilde. To be consulted about anything is a rare experience for her. In the course of the conversation,

Gacougnol invites her to go with him to the zoo where he will make sketches of the animals for his future painting. Enroute there he explains that they will stop to get her a wardrobe. The manner in which he tells her of his plans seems to convey that she is doing him, a surly old man, a favor, rather than he extending himself to her.

> First of all, my dear, you must promise that you'll just let me do as I like without any fuss. I'm one of those creatures who have to be humoured. You came to my place with a view to taking orders from me, I suppose. Consequently, you must just obey me and be very nice about it. You'll understand, I can't take you along with me in that costume.—So we're going to look in at that store we pass on the way, and let you change. Oh, don't worry—it's not a present. I have no right to make you presents. Just a little something on account for our sittings. For one thing, I don't like the poor, you know; can't stick them; my inspiration is too decorative for that. . . .[12]

Such gentle consideration of others' feelings when extending kindness is rarely found. Perhaps only through daily attentiveness and surrender to Christ are we gradually liberated from selfishness and authentically refined in sensibility.

For Francis of Assisi this liberation occurred in one grateful happy moment. Alan Paton tells us that when Francis got down from his horse and embraced the leper, he solved the problem of suffering for himself. In that moment Francis shed all doubt, anxiety and grief over the unsolvable mystery of pain, evil and sorrow; and his whole life was changed. He put himself and his life into God's hands to be made the instrument of God's peace so that he might ease pain, conquer evil and give comfort and strength to the sorrowful. Having detached himself from his suffering-ladened life, Francis was no longer one to suffer and endure, but rather he was one to love and to do.[13]

In conclusion, let us reflect again upon the fact that though faith is God's direct gift to each individual, faith is nurtured in the lonely solitude in which we become more inward. As faith permeates our whole being, we are impelled to follow Christ. To follow means we walk alone and on our own. Judged by the world's standards this following of Christ demands the most intense suffering. Christ does not demand suffering per se. However, once we begin to follow the pattern of Christ, the nature of the world is such that suffering inevitably results since we can no longer evade the call of our authentic religious self and unthinkingly follow the crowd.

Similarly, Dag Hammarskjöld holds that everyone who has made a choice of vocation and "surrendered to it" knows that "the way ends on the Cross."[14] And Ladislas Orsy says,

> The friends of God have always been trained and tested in some sort of desert; it may have been symbolic, it may have been spiritual, but desert it was. It can be by-passed only in the imagination of some, never in reality. Not even Christ by-passed it.[15]

How one friend of God, namely Augustine, deepened in love through suffering is the focus of the next and final chapter.

CHAPTER XII

CHRISTIAN SUFFERING AS LIVED BY AUGUSTINE

". . . our hearts are restless till they rest in Thee."[1]

Augustine's restlessness or disquietude is a characteristic experience of suffering for many people today. Seemingly when physical needs, such as the search for food and shelter, are no longer our prime concern we are, perhaps more conscious of our existence and its accompanying anxiety. How Augustine[2] lives this inner suffering of the spirit and finds rest in Christianity is our focus here.

The most difficult suffering is that which takes place in the inner center of the soul because we live it alone. Herbert Richardson expresses it this way: "Only in our *voluntarily* dying to ourselves in the aloneness of our own spirit can God live in us. The greatest suffering is, therefore, not of the body but of the spirit. This is why it cannot be *seen* by others."[3]

This inner spiritual restlessness about which both Augustine and Richardson speak is also described by the author of *The Cloud of Unknowing* when he refers to the sorrow to which disquietude may lead us:

> Everyone has something to sorrow over, but none more than he who knows and feels that he is. . . . For he experiences true sorrow, who knows and feels not only what he is, but that he is. . . . Such sorrow, when we have it, cleanses the soul not only of sin, but also of the suffering its sin has deserved. And it makes the soul ready to receive that joy

> which is such that it takes from a man all awareness of his own existence . . . When this sorrow is genuine it is full of holy longing. Without such longing no one on earth could cope with it or endure it. For were the soul not strengthened by its good endeavours, it would be unable to stand the pain that the awareness of its own existence brings. . . . This sorrow and longing every soul must know and experience in some form or other.[4]

In our own lives, there are times when we are so involved that we do not feel our separate existence. However, at other times, we experience an inner yearning which seems never to be satisfied—such as in moments when we are lonely, when we have no answers to life's questions or when the absence of the familiar makes us aware of our "own-ness." In a rather helpless way, we seek for "what" we do not know. This elusive inner longing is somewhat indefinable and seemingly unreasonable. In one sense, it is an all-pervasive interior suffering which is often more in the foreground of our consciousness when exterior reality is particularly painful.

We may experience this disquietude when we sense a similar confused cry in another and yet feel unable to either understand or communicate with the other about it. Through the limitations that impinge upon us, we are aware of our bounded existence.

For example, I—You wait with an anxious husband while his wife is having surgery. He tells me that he has tossed and turned all night. Nervously, he fingers his rosary. I look over at him and look away, wondering what I ought to do. My mouth is dry and I have a dull headache. He takes out his handkerchief, turns to me and says, "You know, we never really had any fights. Sometimes we'd be irritable. She's such a good girl, it was always my fault." I utter this platitude, "You wouldn't be human if you didn't have some disagreements." We are quiet for a long while. My headache gets worse and ten minutes seem like an eternity. What should I say? Actions and words—what are they? I want to be there and yet I want to run away. Down the corridor comes a nurse with a newborn baby while a few steps away another's life is in the balance. What is the meaning of it all?

At other times it is hard to know what has triggered this vague anxiety. Many times it is present when we experience a kind of two-way pull in our lives simultaneously, wanting to communicate with another and yet experiencing that much is incommunicable. Perhaps this very vagueness, this inability to understand or convey experience, this apparent aloneness that makes us aware that we are separate and exist over and against or apart from God is what most characterizes disquietude. If the restlessness were not so elusive, if it were one stabbing ache with a definite cause, we might be able to put some order in it, perhaps rationalize it and deal with it. But precisely because it haunts and escapes us so frequently; because we can find no pat and final answer, we may resort to evasion.

We have subtle ways of hiding disquietude, pretending it is not there, putting it away, but it really does not go away. We may ignore our search by perpetual busyness, by losing ourselves in long hours of delightful chatter, or by excessive eating or sleeping. We may act so self assured that we believe we are masters of our situation.

On the other hand, we may realize that it is only in experiencing disquietude that we are cleansed, not only of sin but also of the suffering sin has deserved. In other words, living with disquietude is the passage through it. In thus remaining with our unrest, we experience a calling back, a beckoning home. By dwelling silently with Him who is Truth, we inwardly experience Truth. In the deeper part of ourselves there is a response to this call, that even though we cannot express the mystery of it, we do know what it is to be lovingly held by truth.

To live thus, we must be willing to risk all to faith and to put aside defiant, self-assertive attitudes and await the Truth in the posture of faith, humility and surrender. As has been said in Chapter XI, it is this posture which characterizes the Christian response to suffering: faith in Christ, humility through the awareness of sinfulness and surrender in love.

Hence, the aim here is to ground experientially the concepts discussed in the previous chapter by pondering Augustine's experience of disquietude. Though his experience is uniquely his own, as is that of each person, there are underlying dynamics, the understanding of which, can further our appreciation of the Christian mystery of suffering. For many men the experience of anxiety does not lead to eventual rest in God but only to greater anxiety. Hence, in our anxiety-ridden world, the suffering of disquietude merits reflective thought. Naturally, how we live this mystery will be affected by our individual temperament, our history, our bodily and psychological make-up, as well as, by any number of extenuating circumstances. With this in mind the following points are explored:

1. Augustine's experience of disquietude and the search for faith that this initiates.
2. His recognition of his own sinfulness and the self

knowledge that this imparts.
3. His discovery of God's love in the person of Christ and the joy this can bring to the Christian.

Again, these points further develop the three aspects of suffering considered in this book: 1) exploring my disquietude is an experience of *inwardness,* 2) through which I may recognize my *limitations,* one of which is sin, and 3) awareness that God's love most certainly affects my *attitude* toward the harsher realities of life.

Ralph Harper speaks directly to these truths in relation to Augustine. He says that disquietude or anxiety[5] is my "built-in" image of the cross. It is this restlessness that makes us search. Perhaps only in retrospect, like Augustine, do we realize Who it is we have been seeking.

Specifically, we will consider Harper's insights into the disquietude of Augustine, the need for accepting real sinfulness in ourselves and finally, how we forget our fragmentation through communion with God.

AUGUSTINE'S SEARCH—SORROW AND JOY

Restlessness and the search for faith. According to Harper[6], Augustine is to be characterized almost exclusively by his disquietude. Disquietude is a symptom and an effect of the state of dispersion and fragmentation. To feel oneself split, torn apart and scattered is to reflect a lack of spiritual unity, direction and meaning. Augustine's disquietude had its source in a disobedient will coupled with an intellect seeking faith but dissatisfied with an intellectual answer.

The young Augustine was a God-seeker. He had a goal; but only in retrospect did he know "who" or "what" his goal was. He searched for God in Manichaeism and Platonism and found that he did not want a philosopher's God. He wanted a God to worship, not just a God to know about. He asked the whole frame of the universe about God and it answered, "I am not He, but He made me."[7]

Although Augustine was a God-seeker, he also fled from God—a paradox we frequently experience. For example, at the very moment that our minds are groping with theological and metaphysical questions, our hearts may attach themselves to some part of God's creation. Or, at the very time we respond most deeply to the mystery enshrined in liturgy, we may desire possession of that which distracts us from liturgy.

Man's sinfulness and self knowledge. Augustine was ravished by God's beauty; nonetheless, he was torn from it by carnality. Because of his need for a woman, he found that he was at the end of an elastic leash which pulled him back to a self in strife. Two wills, one spiritual, one carnal, were in conflict and their conflict wasted his soul.

Harper makes some interesting observations regarding the contemporary use of psychoanalysis in man's search for self-knowledge. Had Augustine tried to find himself, as many do today, by undergoing a course in psychoanalysis, it is doubtful whether he would have been converted. Harper says that however much a person comes to know himself through psychoanalysis, it often seems that the more he knows about himself,[8] the less he becomes capable of knowing God.

The agnostic who undergoes psychoanalysis can become acquainted with the origins of his emotional difficulties and may at least come to know what he has repressed and ought to face openly. But if he has never known or felt that holy longing which is the Augustinian disquietude, it is unlikely that psychoanalysis will give him the desire for God. If psychoanalysis could expose in each patient a universal disquietude for the Whole, which could be interpreted to be holy longing, then, says Harper, the role of the priest could begin smoothly from where the psychotherapist left off.[9] Too many who have been psychoanalyzed assume, however, that they know all there is to know about themselves. It is natural that after expense of so much money and so many confidences, they should want to think this. Until a person has become acquainted, however, with his "god-relationship," such self-knowledge is incomplete.

To learn the truth about ourselves and not to learn that God is that truth, that we will always be frustrated until we learn to adore the mystery of love, is to become inadequately acquainted with the dynamic of human nature. When Augustine exhorts us to return to our own hearts that we may find God, he is assuming from his own experience that our heart and the God of that heart are inextricably and mysteriously intertwined.

Not only does "religious psychoanalysis" reach a different conclusion from "medical psychoanalysis"; it also begins with a different assumption, the assumption of sinfulness. Ordinary psychotherapy, on the contrary, begins with a deterministic assumption, namely, that the individual has become so enslaved, so little responsible, that psychotherapy is needed so he may become free. One of the chief signs of freedom is the ability of a person humbly to accept his responsibility for real, not imagined sinfulness.[10]

Love for Christ and neighbor. The whole life of the good Christian is a holy longing. It must be remembered that the longing lonely heart does not seek rest for the sake of rest. Rather, it seeks rest by seeking Christ. Love and longing are not quite the same. Loving worship is more than longing. He who worships does not merely long for union with God. His longing is a desire to bridge the distance between God and himself by love. In communion with God, man's dispersion is forgotten. Wherever Augustine goes—up or down, shamefully or gloriously—love is the gravitational principle, the energy and the direction, the plea for union and recollection.

We must distinguish between a holy and an unholy longing, between the longing for God and the longing for another person. Nevertheless, Augustine is not being heretical when he boldly advises us to look for a real lover, if we are to understand God. This is not to say that we use people for our own selfish ends because every relationship is always an eternal responsibility. However, Augustine's passionate longing for God may have been schooled in his love for the woman whom he sent back to Africa when he was twenty-nine years old. Love of God and love of neighbor are intertwined. If to love our neighbor means that we love him in God, to love God is to feel impelled to become godlike and love our neighbor.

Christ as the Way of life is more than a truth to live by. He is a mystery to be adored and contemplated. He is at one and the same time a paradox of the past, the pattern of the present, and a promise of the future. We cannot comprehend the origin of the paradox, or the power of the pattern, or the glory of the promise but we can believe in it and live by it.

From beginning to end, Harper reminds us, the Augustinian search is an exercise in the intimacy of our being, within which the seeker after rest discovers that there is rest in God, that God is in Christ, and then that the seeker has returned to where he began: the built-in image of the cross—disquietude.

Specifically, let us now reflect on a particular experience described by Augustine during which disquietude is in the foreground of his life.

Reflections on Augustine's Experience

Fragmentation and the awakening of faith. In Book IV of the *Confessions,* Augustine tells of a delightful and intimate friendship. He relates that his friend grew sweeter to him than all the sweetness of life he knew.[11] So close was he to his friend that Augustine felt he could not be without him. But then, quite suddenly his friend dies. Augustine is torn with anguish and he describes his desolate fragmentation as follows:

> Within a few days he relapsed into his fever and died. And I was not there. My heart was black with grief. Whatever I looked upon had the air of death. My native place was a prison house and my home a strange unhappiness. The things we had done together became sheer torment without him. My eyes were restless looking for him, but he was not there. I hated all places because he was not in them. And I could not say "He will come soon", as in his life I could say when he was absent. I became a great enigma to myself and I was forever asking my soul why it was sad and why it disquieted me so sorely.[12]

Without his friend, all things are empty. Augustine is a question to himself. His grief pulls him out of routine ordinariness and starkly confronts him with his separate life. Inwardly he wrestles with his thoughts, feelings, desires and memories. The reality of his anguish is not relieved by a God who is, at this time of his life, foreign to Augustine. Augustine, himself, explains:

> My soul knew not what to answer me. If I said, 'Trust in God' my soul did not obey—naturally, because the man whom she loved and lost was nobler and more real than the imagined deity in whom I was bidding her trust.[13]

Augustine's disquietude is more than a mere painful or momentary state from which he is soon delivered. In the interiority of suffering, he became aware of a self that his former dissipated and distracted life had kept him from knowing. Not having known himself, he has not known God either. Now, as if for the first time, he discovers aspects of himself that are uniquely his own. He glimpses beneath the surface of his exteriorized self and learns the incongruency of what he values. In the aloneness of his grief, he becomes more intimate with himself and understands more clearly the essence of all reality. By being distanced from his friend, he becomes aware of the superficiality of a life bound in "affection for mortal things."

> I was wretched and every soul is wretched that is bound in affection of mortal things: it is tormented to lose them, and in their loss becomes aware of the wretchedness which in reality it had even before it lost them. Such was I at that time . . . I was wretched, yet I held my wretched life dearer than the friend for whose loss I was wretched.[14]

Such intense awareness is seldom experienced independent of suffering. Bearing with disquietude can free the spirit and center one in true selfness in a way in which no other experience can. In this inwardness, Augustine penetrated to the very roots of his life and is awakened to his complacency. In the lines which follow he describes his inability to find peace or joy in former satisfying distractions:

> I raged and sighed and wept and was in torment, unable to rest, unable to think. I bore my soul all broken and bleeding and loathing to be borne by me; and I could find nowhere to set it down to rest. Not in shady groves, nor in mirth and music, nor in perfumed gardens, nor in formal banquets, nor in the delights of bedroom and bed, not in books nor in poetry could it find peace. I hated all things, hated the very light itself; and all that was painful and wearisome, save only my tears; for in them alone did I find a little peace.[15]

This painful inward experience in which he searches for rest nourishes Augustine's spirit. His dissatisfaction with former distractions somewhat distances him from his vital or biopsychic life and from his public life, as well. In the interiority of his person, he becomes aware of the "lumen naturale" that he is. His interiority is readied to be illuminated and transformed by grace and revelation. Augustine's receptivity to the gift of grace is the means by which his desolation is transfigured. Faith is reawakened.

When Augustine had little or no faith, bidding his soul to trust in God was meaningless. For example, in the earlier quote, Augustine refers to God as "the imagined deity."

Hopelessly, he endures his friend's death with self-pity, panic and rebellion. Gradually, as Augustine reflects upon his life, his faith incarnates itself in his vital life. He is able to unite his will with the will of God and thus his faith becomes a lived faith. God becomes real for him. Slowly, through the years his spiritual life deepens. Augustine's reflections in the following selection evidence his growing faith. Here he shows that faith does not depend on explanations and that all ought to be committed to God, because it is dependent on Him for existence and will thus fulfill its purpose:

> Blessed is the man that loves Thee, O God, and his friend in Thee, and his enemy for Thee. For he alone loses no one that is dear to him, if all are dear in God, who is never lost . . . Wherever the soul of man turns unless towards God, it cleaves to sorrow, even though the things outside itself to which it cleaves may be things of beauty. For these lovely things would be nothing at all unless they were from Him . . . Things pass that other things may come in their place . . . Fix your dwelling in Him, commit to God whatsoever you have: for it is from God. O my soul, wearied at last with emptiness, commit to Truth's keeping whatever you have of truth, and you shall not lose any.[16]

Sinfulness and Augustine's growing love for Christ. In his grief Augustine is unable to do anything to change his situation. He must accept his limitation. He realizes that he is dependent and sinful. Throughout the *Confessions* his sinfulness is acknowledged for what it is, a love of sin. Augustine does not rationalize or deny that he is sinful and therefore guilty. He lives passionately and he knows his own barrenness, as well as, his fullness. His is not an unaware mediocre existence. He admits that he finds it difficult to love a God who sends sickness and death. Though in later life he finds an answer in the person of Christ, who calls Augustine through death to Resurrection:

> You seek happiness of life in the land of death, and it is not there. For how shall there be happiness of life where there is no life? But our life came down to this our earth and took away our death, slew death with the abundance of His own life; and He thundered, calling us to return to Him into that secret place from which He came forth to us—coming first into the Virgin's womb, where humanity was wedded to Him, our mortal flesh, though not always to be mortal; and thence 'like a bridegroom coming out of his bride chamber, rejoicing as a giant to run his course'. For He did not delay, but rushed on, calling to us by what He said, and what He did, calling to us by His death, life, descent, and ascension to return to Him. And He withdrew from our eyes that we might return to our own heart and find Him.[17]

To be inspired by the person of Christ, the God-man must be encountered. Augustine says that He is found by looking within. Suffering because of the interiority which it fosters, facilitates this return to the heart. John Tauler, a German Dominican mystic, reiterates this invitation by emphasizing the Gospel counsel which speaks of finding God within.

> We must go into our own souls, into the very depths, and seek the Lord there, as He counselled us when He said: 'The kingdom of God is within you!' Anyone who wants to find this kingdom—that is, to find God, with all His riches and in His own being and nature—must look for it where it is, in the very depths of his soul, where God is infinitely closer to the soul and more integral to it than is the soul to itself.[18]

John Tauler, like some of the psychologists of today, though from a different perspective, also emphasizes the importance of living and experiencing suffering so that it may bear fruit. To truly find Christ within is to take up the cross with Him. Tauler insists on this necessity in the following words which are taken from his sermon on Corpus Christi:

> Also, do not run away from yourself. It is a thousand times more profitable for you to see this through than it would be to read a great number of books or to do anything else which might help you to escape from this affliction. On the other hand you should be on your guard at such times lest your enemy the devil should smite you with immoderate melancholy. He would like to serve you with bitter herbs: but the herbs which our Lord puts before you are sweet and wholesome, and when He has chastised you, your whole mind will be sweet-savored. You will have loving faith in Him, from confidence and childlike hope.[19]

The sweetness to which Tauler refers is a kind of joy—the

joy that follows upon surrender in love. Here we present two examples which show the personal relation between joy and suffering: one taken from the life of Bishop Leonard Wilson and the other from the life of Saint Francis as presented in Kazantzakis' literary work by that title.

In 1946, Leonard Wilson, then Bishop of Singapore, talked on the radio of his experiences as a Japanese prisoner of war:

> I speak to you this morning from personal experience of God's comfort and strength. I was interned by the Japanese; I was imprisoned by their militant police for many months; I suffered many weary hours of beatings and torture . . . It is not my purpose to relate the tortures . . . but rather to tell you of some of the spiritual experiences of that ordeal . . . It is true that there were many dreary moments . . . There was a tiny window at the back of the cell, and through the bars I could hear the song of the Golden Oriole. I could see the glorious red of the flame of the forest tree; and something of God, something of God's indestructible beauty, was conveyed to my tortured mind . . . After eight months I was released, and for the first time got into the sunlight. I have never known such joy. It seemed like a foretaste of the Resurrection. For months afterwards I felt at peace with the universe. . . . God is to be found in the Resurrection, as well as in the Cross, and it is the Resurrection that has the final word.[20]

Joy and suffering in Bishop Wilson's life were not mutually exclusive but rather compatible. He came to know joy through suffering and suffering through joy. Such is the rhythm of life. The seed must die so that it may be born. To save our lives we must lose them. Painful death may be the prelude to glorious rebirth.

St. Francis as presented by Nikos Kazantzakis seems also to have experienced his suffering in a joyful manner. Francis says, "I weep, I laugh, and weeping and laughing are the same thing."[21] And Brother Leo says of Francis,

> Though he did not know it, he was like the leprous king of Jerusalem—a handful of flesh and bone, with God, God in His entirety, sitting inside. That was why he could endure, why he never felt hunger or thirst or cold, why the stones which people threw at him were like a sprinkling of leon flowers.[22]

Again Francis says to Leo,

> When a person believes in God there is no such thing as a mute piece of wood, or pain unaccompanied by exultation, or ordinary everyday life without miracles![23]

For Francis suffering did seem to be a form of joy.

For Francis' life was patterned on that of Christ. Christ's life does not eliminate suffering nor does it provide a final solution to suffering. His life, however, must become an essential element in our Christian response. We can accept suffering as Christ accepted it, that is, as devastatingly real but not necessarily as hopelessly final. He has risen and in the Resurrection is our hope.

EPILOGUE

It is Holy Week, I sit in the back of chapel, hearing the wind whistle in a rather low tone, getting louder and then quieting softly. It seems the wind has gone; but, no, it returns following the same cycle. The morning sun makes slanted long rectangles on the floor. Interiorly I am quiet, far away a bird chirps . . . He is here, always here, always He holds me up and that is the strength of suffering.

More than anything, my greatest suffering seems to be the fear of suffering but as I feel His strength about me, this fear leaves. At least temporarily I freely live in the present. The birds sound closer to the chapel windows. Listening to them I begin to wonder if I am eavesdropping on private though animated conversation. I cannot write a conclusion to the suffering question. I have no answers and perhaps that is as it should be.

In fact, I feel I have not even begun to scratch the surface of the deep mystery of suffering, of life. In one way I can identify with the child at the base of a long stairway continually lifting its foot and yet not ever quite making the first step. Perhaps it is in not giving up the attempt that someday I will be lifted and taken to the top.

There is much I could explore about suffering. But even had I lived the lives of all the men who have gone before me and who are to follow after, it seems I still would live in shadow and be in awe before mystery . . . The wind is almost inaudible now and the birds too, are still.

Suffering remains a mystery and I am glad, knowing mystery abides, so too does beauty, love, surprise and joy.

FOOTNOTES

PART I

CHAPTER I

1. Dag Hammarskjöld, *Markings,* trans. W.H. Auden and Leif Sjöberg (New York: Alfred A. Knopf, 1969), p. 58.

PART II

CHAPTER II

1. John W. Gardner, *Self Renewal* (New York: Harper and Row, 1965), p. 9.

Also refer to Anthony T. Padovano, *America: Its People, Its Promise* (Cincinnati: St. Anthony Messenger Press, 1975), pp. 46-48. Discusses mobility for Americans as manna in the desert for our restless spirit and as a narcotic when the stress of stability becomes unbearable.

2. R.D. Laing, *The Politics of Experience* (New York: Ballantine Books, 1967), p. 167.

3. We do not wish to imply that healthy defenses are not necessary. Rather, slavery to unrecognized defensive behavior is often the basis of needless suffering.

4. Karen Horney, *Neurosis and Human Growth* (New York: W.W. Norton and Co., Inc., 1950) and *The Neurotic Personality of Our Time* (New York: W.W. Norton & Co., Inc., 1937), pp. 1-29, 259-280.

5. Paraphrased from Envoy (Published by the Institute of Man, Duquesne University), September, 1971, Question of the Month.

CHAPTER III

1. In many instances individual men may never have found selfhood and hence it is not necessarily lost. However, in the sense that man has a whole history and that each is unique, "losing selfhood" seems to be a legitimate way of stating the present alienation.

2. David Reisman, *The Lonely Crowd* (New Haven: Yale University Press, 1961 book jacket).

3. Thornton Wilder, *Eight Day* (New York: Harper and Row Publishers, 1967).

4. Clark E. Moustakas, *Loneliness* (Englewood Cliffs: Prentice-Hall, Inc., 1961), p. 24.

5. Desmond Morris, *The Human Zoo* (New York: McGraw-Hill Book Co., 1969), p. 8.

6. John H. Griffin, *Black Like Me* (Boston: Houghton Mifflin Co., 1960).

7. Benjamin Epstein and Arnold Foster, *Some of My Best Friends* (New York: Farrar, Straus and Cudahy, 1962).

8. John Grimes, *When Minds Go Wrong* (New York: Devin-Adair Company, 1954).

9. Edgar May, *The Wasted Americans* (New York: Harper and Row, 1964).

10. Graham Greene, *A Burnt Out Case* (New York: Viking Press, 1961), p. 12.

11. *Ibid.*, p. 191.

12. *Ibid.*, p. 151.

13. *Ibid.*, p. 220.

14. *Ibid.*, p. 232.

15. *Ibid.*, p. 241.

16. See Adrian van Kaam, *On Being Yourself: Reflections on*

Spirituality and Originality (Denville, N.J.: Dimension Books, 1972).

17. See Adrian van Kaam, Bert van Croonenburg, Susan Muto, *The Emergent Self* (Denville, N.J.: Dimension Books, 1968).

PART III

CHAPTER IV

1. Jean Vieujean, *Love, Suffering, Providence,* trans. Joan M. Roth (Westminster: Newman Press, 1964), Frontispiece.

2. Louis Lavelle, *Evil and Suffering,* trans. Bernard Murchland (New York: MacMillan Co., 1963), pp. 74-76.

3. Viktor E. Frankl, *The Doctor and the Soul,* trans. Richard and Clara Winston (New York: Alfred A. Knopf, 1965), pp. 107-111.

4. Viktor Frankl, one of Europe's leading psychiatrists, is well qualified to discuss the importance of man's attitude in actualizing the value of suffering. He himself was a longtime prisoner in several Nazi concentration camps where he suffered from hunger, cold, exhaustion and brutality. There he lost his every possession including the manuscript to his book and faced the constant imminence of death. Except for his sister, his entire family died in the gas chambers. Stripped to his naked existence, Frankl could still find meaning in his sufferings. He became neither pessimistic nor anti-religious but took a surprisingly hopeful view of man's capacity to transcend his situation and to discover the truth. (Taken from Viktor E. Frankl, *Man's Search for Meaning,* trans. Ilse Lasch (New York: Washington Square Press, 1963), Preface ix-x).

5. Viktor E. Frankl, *The Will To Meaning* (Cleveland: The World Publishing Co., 1969), p. 51.

6. This healthy striving is not to be confused with excessive idealization which accompanies the neurotic conflict described in Chapter Two.

7. Frankl, *Man's Search for Meaning, op. cit.,* pp. 164-167.

8. *Ibid.,* pp. 160-164; 167-171. Frankl, *The Will to Meaning op. cit.,* pp. 46-47; Frankl, *The Doctor and the Soul, op. cit.,* p. 109.

9. Jean Piaget emphasis the fact that what a person really learns is actually a part of the logical operation of that person so that it is practically impossible to separate man and his learning. In other words, every content studied develops a form of living, as well. (See Jean Piaget, *Science of Education and the Psychology of the Child,* trans. Derek Coltman (New York: Orion Press, 1970).

10. The word "identify" could be misleading. We do not use "identify" in the sense that one "identifies" in empathizing with another but rather "identifying" refers to a mere passive complacent, and unfeeling way of dealing with the harsher realities of life.

11. Erich Fromm and Ramon Xirau (eds.), *The Nature of Man* (New York: MacMillan, 1968), p. 151.

CHAPTER V

1. Kahil, Gibran, *The Prophet,* (New York: Alfred A. Knopf, 1955), p. 29.

2. Lavelle, *op. cit.,* p. 77.

3. Though Nolting uses the term "happiness", his meaning is similar to that of the joy to which reference is made here.

4. W.J.J. de Sauvage Nolting, M.D., "The Meaning of Suffering," *Existential Psychiatry,* VI (XXVIII, 1970), p. 75-86.

5. Ladislaus Boros, *Meeting God In Man,* trans. Wm. Glen-Doepel (New York: Herder and Herder, 1968), pp. 43-45.

6. Nolting, *op. cit.*, p. 76; also see James Lord, *A Giocometti Portrait* (New York: 1964), p. 26 for further development of this thought.

7. *Ibid.*, citing A. Schweitzer, *Das Christentum und Die Weltreligionen.*

8. Herman Hesse, *Narcissus and Goldmund,* trans. Ursule Molinaro (New York: Farrar, Straus and Giroux, 1969), p. 53

9. *Ibid.*, p. 149.

10. Ibid., p. 149.

11. *Ibid.*, p. 152.

12. *Ibid.*, p. 165.

13. *Ibid.*, p. 203.

14. *Ibid.*, p. 308.

15. *Ibid.*, p. 206.

16. Lavelle, *op. cit.*, pp. 80-81.

CHAPTER VI

1. Lavelle, *op. cit.*, pp. 82-83.

2. Rollo May, *The Courage to Create,* (New York: W.W. Norton and Co., Inc., 1975), p. 25.

3. Bernard Malamud, *A Malamud Reader* (New York: Farrar, Straus and Giroux, 1967), pp. 480-481.

4. See Adrian van Kaam, *Spirituality and the Gentle Life* (Denville, N.J.: Dimension Books, 1974).

4. *Ibid.*, p. 487.

5. *Ibid.*

CHAPTER VII

1. Lavelle, *op. cit.* pp. 84-89.

2. Rollo, May, *Man's Search for Himself* (New York: W.W. Norton Co., 1953), p. 60.

3. Dag Hammarskjöld, *Markings,* trans. W.H. Auden and Leif Sjöberg (London: Faber and Faber, 1964), p. 63.

4. James Collins, *The Existentialists* (Chicago: Henry Regnery Co., 1952), p. 161.

CHAPTER VIII

1. William Wordsworth, "My Heart Leaps Up When I Behold" in *The Pocket Book of Verse,* ed. M.E. Speare (New York: Washington Square Press, Inc., 1940), p. 103.

2. William Blake, "The Tiger" in *The Pocket Book of Verse, op. cit.,* p. 85.

3. Collins, *op. cit.,* pp. 128-167.

4. Alfred Lord Tennyson, "Flower in the Crannied Wall" in *The Pocket Book of Verse, op. cit.,* p. 222.

5. William Blake, "Auguries of Innocence" in *The Pocket Book of Verse, op. cit.,* p. 86.

6. See Adrian van Kaam, *Personality Fulfillment in the Spiritual Life* (Denville, N.J.: Dimension Books, 1966) for a fuller development of man's openness to mystery.

CHAPTER IX

1. For a further discussion of these dynamics refer to Alasdair Mac Intyre and Paul Ricoeur, *The Religious Significance of Atheism* (New York: Columbia U. Press, 1969).

2. We may be inclined to look upon myth as mere myth and

hence question the validity of using mythology to indicate a distortion of religious suffering. However, since these mythical characters are the creations of man's mind, they evidence the way man perceives God's relation to the world.

3. H.J. Rose, *Religion in Greece and Rome* (New York: Harper and Brothers, 1959), pp. 15-16.

4. Homer, *The Illiad,* trans. W.H.D. Rouse (New York: New American Library, 1954), p. 213.

5. *Ibid.,* p. 230.

6. Dorothy M. Johnson, *A Man Called Horse* (New York: Ballantine Books, 1953), p. 144.

7. W. Somerset Maugham, *Of Human Bondage* (New York: Pocket Books, Inc., 1950), p. 17.

8. *Ibid.,* p. 59.

9. I do not wish to negate the necessity of always living in tune with God's Will. The purpose here, however, is to indicate the manner in which we may credit to God that which is merely our own will, thus escaping responsibility for making constructive efforts to improve our life situation, or the way in which we use "God's Will" to manipulate others into doing our will.

10. Thomas Merton, *No Man Is An Island* (New York: Dill Publishers, 1955), p. 91.

11. In a rather lengthy footnote let us comment on responses to suffering as they are somewhat distinct in the major religions of the world today.

In Judaism, suffering is seen as a penalty for sin. It can be made redemptive and become the foundation of better things collectively, if not individually. Suffering is a way of grace and atonement.

The Christian response to suffering is similar to that of the Jews. Man is redeemed by the sacrificial suffering of Christ who is God's love made incarnate. The Christian understanding of suffering is developed in the areas of explanation and practice.

These concepts are more fully considered in Part IV of this book.

In the Ismalic view, suffering is a punishment for sin and an instrument for God's purposes. It is a spiritual trial or test and in this sense, suffering forms man's character and reveals his true nature.

Suffering for the Hindus is an experience of reality from a special and limited perspective. It is real enough but it must be seen in relation to the whole. Brahman pervades all without being exhausted in any one. Suffering is not the final truth about existence. The danger of this view is that one may become indifferent to the removal of human distress.

The Buddhist term, "dukka" refers to impermanence, emptiness and a lack of wholeness. From all this man seeks to escape into the reality of nirvana. The ideal is to postpone one's own escape in order to help his fellows to salvation. Hence, Buddhism contains within itself a tremendous ideal of compassion and of self-giving for others.

There is agreement among the religions of the world. All consider suffering as a real and grievous experience. All see suffering as that which can be turned into a pathway which leads to the transcendent good, of heaven, or Brahman, or nirvana. All see good as final and evil as provisional. (For a more thorough discussion of the above refer to the book from which this was taken—John Bowker, *Problems of Suffering in the Religions of the World* (Cambridge: Cambridge University Press, 1970).

CHAPTER X

1. Albert Gelin, *The Poor of Yahweh,* trans. Kathryn Sullivan (Collegeville: The Liturgical Press, 1964), p. 46 citing Gabriel Marcel, *Le Chemin de Crete,* p. 174.

2. Jean Vieujean, *Love, Suffering, Providence,* trans. Joan Marie Roth (Westminster: The Newman Press, 1964), p. 73.

3. France Pastorelli, *Strength Out Of Suffering* (a translation

of Grandeur de la Maladie (New York: Houghton Mifflin Co., 1936), pp. 91-92.

4. *Ibid.*, pp. 87-98.

5. Gordon W. Allport, *The Individual and His Religion* (London: Collier, MacMillan Limited, 1950), p. 53.

6. C.S. Lewis, *The Problem of Pain* (New York: Macmillan, 1961), p. 14.

7. Vieujean, *op. cit.*, pp. 79-87.

8. Lewis, *op. cit.*, p. 21.

9. All direct references taken from F.T. Prince (ed.), *Milton's Samson Agonistes* (London: Oxford University Press, 1965). For further development see F. Michael Krouse, *Milton's Samson and the Christian Tradition* (Princeton: Princeton University Press, 1949), pp. 22-79.

CHAPTER XI

1. Thomas Merton, *No Man Is An Island* (New York: Dell Pub., 1951), p. 96.

2. *Ibid.*, pp. 11-21; 91-106.

3. Francis Thompson, "The Hound of Heaven" (Philadelphia: Peter Reilly Co., 1926), p. 23 (lines 1-4).

4. *The Prayers of Kierkegaard,* ed. Perry D. Lefevre (Chicago: University of Chicago Press, 1956), p. 36.

5. Ladislaus Boros, Pain and Providence, trans. Edward Quinn (Baltimore: Helicon, 1965), p. 121.

6. To compassionate is to "suffer with." Perhaps why we seldom live in a compassionate manner is explained by Elizabeth Goudge in the novel, *The Scent of Water.* Here she has Mary remark, "Most of us tend to belittle all suffering but our own. I think it's fear. We don't want to come too near in case we're

sucked in and have to share it." (New York: Pyramid, 1963), p. 30.

7. Leon Bloy, *The Woman Who Was Poor,* trans. I.J. Collins (New York: Sheed and Ward, 1939), p. 51.

8. *Ibid.,* pp. 53-54.

9. *Ibid.,* p. 54.

10. *Ibid.,* pp. 54-55.

11. *Ibid.,* p. 55.

12. *Ibid.,* p. 60.

13. Alan Paton and others, *Creative Suffering* (Kansas City: National Catholic Reporter, 1970), p. 16.

14. Dag Hammarskjöld, *Markings,* trans. W.H. Auden and Leif Sjöberg (London: Faber and Faber, 1964), p. 88.

15. Ladislas Örsy, *Open to the Spirit* (Washington, D.C.: Corpus Books, 1968), p. 91.

CHAPTER XII

1. Aurelius Augustinus, *Confessions of St. Augustine,* trans. F.J. Sheed (New York: Sheed and Ward, 1942), p. 3.

2. We refer to Augustine because experientially the characteristics of Augustine's search correlate with the dynamics of Christian suffering which were discussed in Chapter XI. Also John Bowker in studying man's response to suffering in the various religions of the world refers to Augustine as one who has profoundly influenced Christian thought with regard to suffering.) *Problems of Suffering in the Religions of the World* (Cambridge: University Press, 1970), p. 84 citing John Hick, *Evil and the God of Love* (London: 1966).

3. Alan Paton and others, *Creative Suffering* (Kansas City: National Catholic Reporter Publishing, 1970), p. 119.

4. Author unknown, *The Cloud of Unknowing,* trans. Clifton

Wolters (Middlesex, England: Penguin, 1961), pp. 104-105.

5. Here, like Harper, we use anxiety and disquietude synonymously, though it should be pointed out that there are various types and degrees of anxiety. The anxiety to which we refer here might be called the "anxiety of the cross" which according to Wayne Oates, is a creative uneasiness of spirit. In its ultimate dimension, Oates refers to anxiety as holy dread, a stance in which the Christian awaits the reconciliation that proceeds from the mind of God in Christ. For further discussion of the distinctions in regard to anxiety see Wayne E. Oates, *Anxiety in Christian Experience* (Philadelphia: Westminster, 1952).

6. Ralph Harper, *The Seventh Solitude* (Baltimore: John Hopkins, 1965), pp. 114-153.

7. Augustinus, *op. cit.,* p. 216.

8. Note here that Harper states *about* himself. It would seem that he is referring to an objectivated attitude toward the self.

9. It could quite rightly be argued that the role of psychoanalysis is not to expose "universal disquietude." Harper's stand here is controversial. He limits his observation, however, to psychoanalysis, so it would seem that he is not including the whole field of psychotherapy. Harper contributes to our considerations by reminding us that true self-knowledge includes more than self-knowledge acquired through psychoanalysis.

10. These excerpts from a personal letter, experientially speak of one person's concern that sin might be written off.

> "I am seeing a psychologist and he is teaching me to talk in pencil and its kinda fun. I pursue myself as far as I want and if I don't like it I just erase it. . . .
> One of the fears hanging over my "sessions" with the pencil thinker is that he will get me to believe that sin is sickness. In a sense it is. But sin is sin, too. I am learning something new about that. If there is any wisdom in 2,000 years of Christianity, that should be one of the

premises from which to draw some strength: "I'm a sinner."

11. Augustinus, *op. cit.*, p. 65.

12. *Ibid.*, p. 66.

13. *Ibid.*

14. *Ibid.*, p. 67.

15. *Ibid.*, p. 68.

16. Augustinus, *op. cit.*, pp. 70-71.

17. *Ibid.*, p. 73.

18. Johannes Tauler, *Spiritual Conferences,* trans. and eds. Eric Colledge and Sister M. Jane (St. Louis: B Herder, 1961), p. 32.

19. *Ibid.*, p. 101.

20. Bowker, *op. cit.*, p. 94 citing E.L. Mascall, *Grace and Glory* (London: 1961), pp. 20f.

21. Nikos Kazantzakis, Saint Francis, trans. P.A. Bien (New York: Ballantine Books, 1962), p. 75.

22. *Ibid.*, p. 121.

23. *Ibid.*, p. 414.

SELECTED BIBLIOGRAPHY

Primary Sources

Books

Augustinus, Aurelius. *The Confessions of St. Augustine.* Trans. F.J. Sheed. New York: Sheed and Ward, 1942.

Bakan, David. *Disease, Pain, and Sacrifice: Toward a Psychology of Suffering.* Chicago: The University of Chicago, 1968.

Bonhoeffer, Dietrich. *Letters and Papers from Prison.* Edited by Eberhard Bethge. London: SCM Press, 1967.

Boros, Ladislaus. *Meeting God in Man.* Trans. William Glen-Doepel. New York: Herder and Herder, 1968.

Bowker, John. *Problems of Suffering in Religions of the World.* Cambridge: Cambridge University Press, 1970.

Eliot, T.S. *Murder in the Cathedral.* New York: Harcourt, Brace and World, Inc., 1935.

Frankl, Viktor. *The Doctor and the Soul: From Psychotherapy to Logotherapy.* Trans. Richard and Clara Winston. New York: Alfred A. Knopf, 1965.

________. *Man's Search for Meaning.* Trans. Ilse Lasch. New York: Washington Square Press, 1963.

________. *The Will to Meaning.* Cleveland: The World Publishing Co., 1969.

Greene, Graham. *A Burnt-Out Case.* New York: The Viking Press, 1961.

Horney, Karen. *Neurosis and Human Growth.* New York: W.W. Norton, 1950.

Josephson, Eric and Mary (eds.). *Man Alone: Alienation in Modern Society.* New York: Dell Publishing Co., 1962.

Kazantzakis, Nikos. *Saint Francis.* Trans. P.A. Bien. New York: Ballantine Books, 1962.

Kierkegaard, Sren. *Gospel of Our Suffering.* Trans. A.S.

Aldsworth and W.S. Ferrie. Grand Rapids, Michigan: William B. Eerdmans Publishing Co., 1964.

Lavelle, Louis. *Evil and Suffering.* Trans. Bernard Murchland. New York: Macmillan, 1963.

Marcel, Gabriel. *Being and Having.* Trans. Katherine Farrar. New York: Harper and Row Publishers, 1965.

May, Rollo. *Man's Search for Himself.* New York: W.W. Norton and Company, 1953.

Merton, Thomas. *No Man Is An Island.* New York: Dell, 1955.

Milton, John. *Samson Agonistes.* Edited by F.T. Prince. London: Oxford University Press, 1957.

Moustakas, Clark E. *Loneliness.* Englewood Cliffs, New Jersey: Prentice-Hall, Inc., 1961.

Oraison, Marc. *Illusion and Anxiety.* New York: Macmillan Co., 1963.

Riesman, David. *The Lonely Crowd.* New Haven: Yale University Press, 1961.

Rumke, H.C. *The Psychology of Unbelief.* Trans. M.H. C. Willems. New York: Sheed and Ward, 1949.

Unamuno, y Jugo, Miguel de. *Tragic Sense of Life.* Trans. J.E. Crawford Flitch. New York: Dover Publications, 1954.

van Kaam, Adrian. *Religion and Personality.* Englewood Cliffs, New Jersey: Prentice-Hall, Inc., 1964.

Vieujean, Jean. *Love, Suffering, Providence.* Trans. Joan Roth. Westminster: The Newman Press, 1964.

Zeller, Hubert van. *Suffering in Other Words.* Springfield: Templegate Publishers, 1964.

Secondary Sources

Books

Agee, James. *A Death in the Family.* New York: McDowell, Obolensky, 1957.

Ahern, Barnabas M. *New Horizons.* Edited by Carroll Stuhlmueller. Notre Dame: Fides Publishers, Inc., 1963.

Ardrey, Robert. *African Genesis.* New York: Atheneum, 1967.

_______. *The Territorial Imperative.* New York: Atheneum, 1966.

Bernanos, Georges. *The Diary of a Country Priest.* New York: The Macmillan Co., 1937.

Bertangs, A. *The Bible on Suffering.* Trans. F. Vander Heyden. DePere, Wisconsin: St. Norbert Abbey Press, 1966.

Biddle, W. Earl. *Integration of Religion and Psychiatry.* New York: Collier Books, 1955.

Bonhoeffer, Dietrich. *The Way To Freedom.* Edited by Edwin H. Robinson. New York: Harper and Row, 1966.

Boros, Ladislaus. *Mystery of Death.* New York: Herder and Herder, 1965.

Brown, Wallace L. *The Endless Hours: My Two and a Half Years as a Prisoner of the Chinese Communists.* New York: Norton, 1961.

Burney, Christopher. *Solitary Confinement.* New York: St. Martin's Press, 1961.

Camus, Albert. *The Plague.* Trans. Stuart Gilbert. New York: Alfred A. Knopf, 1960.

_______. *Resistance, Rebellion and Death.* Trans. Justin O'Brien. New York: Alfred A. Knopf, 1961.

Delp, Alfred. *Facing Death.* Bloomsbury: Bloomsbury Publishing Cor., Ltd., 1962.

Duquoc, Christian (ed.). "Concilium Theology in the Age of Renewal." Vol. XXXIX. *The Gift of Joy.* New York: Paulist Press, 1968.

Durwell, F.X. *In the Redeeming Christ.* Trans. Rosemary Sheed. New York: Sheed and Ward, 1963.

_______. *The Resurrection.* New York: Sheed and Ward, 1960.

Dusenbury, Winifred L. *Theme of Loneliness in Modern American Drama.* Gainesville, Florida: University of Florida Press, 1960.

Eliot, T.S. *The Cocktail Party.* New York: Harcourt, Brace and World, Inc., 1950.

Evely, Louis. *Joy*. Trans. Brian and Marie-Claude Thompsen. New York: Herder and Herder, 1968.

________. *Suffering*. Trans. Marie-Claude Thompsen. New York: Herder and Herder, 1967.

Frankel, Charles. *The Love of Anxiety and Other Essays*. New York: Harper and Row, 1951.

Fromm, Erich. *The Art of Loving*. New York: Bantam Books, 1956.

________. *The Revolution of Hope*. New York: Bantam Books, Inc., 1968.

________. *War Within Man: A Psychological Inquiry into the Roots of Destructiveness*. Philadelphia: American Friends Service Committee, 1963.

Harper, Ralph. *Path of Darkness*. Cleveland: Press of Case-Western Reserve University, 1968.

Heschel, Abraham Joshua. *Who Is Man?* Stanford, California: Stanford University Press, 1965.

Hesse, Herman. *Siddhartha*. Trans. Hilda Rossner. New York: New Directions Publishing Company, 1951.

Houselander, Caryll. *The Risen Christ*. New York: Sheed and Ward, 1958.

Jaspers, Karl. *Tragedy Is Not Enough*. Boston: Beacon Press, 1952.

John of the Cross. *Dark Night of the Soul*. Trans. E. Allison Peers. Garden City: Doubleday and Co., Inc., 1959.

Kerr, Walter. *The Decline of Pleasure*. New York: Simon and Schuster, 1962.

Klein, Melanie and Joan Riviere. *Love, Hate, and Reparation*. New York: Norton, 1964.

Kraus, Ota Benjamin and Erich Julka. *The Death Factory: Document on Auschwitz*. Trans. Stephen Jolly. Oxford: Pergamon Press, 1966.

Kuber-Ross, Elisabeth. *On Death and Dying*. New York: Macmillan Co., 1969.

Lefebvre, Dom Georges. *The Mystery of God's Love*. Trans. Geoffrey Chapman. London: Catholic Book Club, 1957.

Lepp, Ignace. *The Challenges of Life.* Staten Island, New York: Alba House, 1969.

Lotz, Johannes B. *Problem of Loneliness.* New York: Alba House, 1967.

Malin, Irving. *Jews and Americans.* Carbondale and Edwardsville: Southern Illinois University Press, 1965.

Malamud, Bernard. *The Fixer.* New York: Farrar, Straus and Giroux, 1966.

Maritain, Jacques. *St. Thomas and the Problem of Evil.* Milwaukee: Marquette, 1942.

Marmion, Columba. *Christ in His Mysteries.* Trans. Mother M. St. Thomas. 10th ed. St. Louis: B. Herder Book Co., 1939.

May, Rollo. *Love and Will.* New York: W.W. Norton and Company, Inc., 1969.

________. *The Meaning of Anxiety.* New York: The Ronald Press Company, 1950.

Montagu, Ashley. *The Humanization of Man.* New York: Grove Press, Inc., 1962.

________. *On Being Human.* New York: Hawthorn Books, Inc., 1966.

Neibuhr, Reinhold. *Beyond Tragedy.* New York: Charles Scribner's Sons, 1955.

Pasternak, Boris. *Doctor Zhivago.* Trans. Max Hayward and Manya Harari. New York: The New America Library, 1958.

Petrie, Asenath. *Individuality in Pain and Suffering.* Chicago: University of Chicago, 1967.

Reik, Theodor. *Myth and Guilt.* New York: George Braziller, Inc., 1957.

Ricoeur, Paul. *Fallible Man.* Trans. Charles Kebbley. Chicago: Regnery, 1965.

________. *Symbolism of Evil.* New York: Harper and Row, Publishers, 1967.

Royce, Josiah. *Studies of Good and Evil: A Series of Essays Upon Problems of Philosophy and of Life.* Hamden, Connecticut: Shoe String Press, Inc., 1898.

Sartre, John-Paul. *Being and Nothingness.* Trans. Hazel E. Barnes. New York: Citadel Press, 1968.

Schutz, William C. *Joy: Expanding Human Awareness.* New York: Grove Press, 1967.

Sternbach, Richard A. *Pain: A Psychophysiological Analysis.* New York: Academic Press, 1968.

Stolpe, Sven. Dag Hammarskjöld: *A Spiritual Portrait.* New York: Charles Scribner and Sons, 1966.

Thoreau, Henry. *Walden.* New York: New American Library, 1960.

Tournier, Paul. *The Strong and the Weak.* Trans. Edwin Hudson. Philadelphia: The Westminster Press, 1963.

van Croonenburg, Engelbert J. *Gateway to Reality: An Introduction to Philosophy.* Pittsburgh: Duquesne University Press, 1963.

van Kaam, Adrian. *Personality Fulfillment in the Spiritual Life.* Denville, N.J.: Dimension Books, 1966.

________. *On Being Yourself: Reflections on Spirituality and Originality.* Denville, N.J.: Dimension Books, 1972.

________. *Spirituality and the Gentle Life.* Denville, N.J.: Dimension Books, 1972.

van Kaam, Adrian, Bert van Cronenburg, Susan Muto. *The Emergent Self.* Denville, N.J.: Dimension Books, 1968.

Vann, Gerald. *The Divine Pity.* New York: Sheed and Ward, 1946.

________. *Of His Fullness.* New York: P.J. Kenedy and Sons, 1939.

Watts, Alan Wilson. *The Wisdom of Insecurity.* New York: Pantheon, 1951.

Weaver, Bertrand. *Joy.* New York: Sheed and Ward, 1964.

Wellek, Rene (ed.). Dostoevsky: *A Collection of Critical Essays.* Englewood Cliffs, New Jersey: Prentice-Hall, Inc., 1962.

Yarmolinsky, Avrahm. *Dostoevsky, His Life and Art.* New York: Criterion Books, 1957.

Zeller, Hubert van. *Approach to Calvary.* New York: Sheed and Ward, 1961.

________. *The Inner Search.* New York: Sheed and Ward, 1957.